THE HAMLYN LECTURES
FORTIETH SERIES

JUSTIFICATION AND EXCUSE
IN
THE CRIMINAL LAW

AUSTRALIA AND NEW ZEALAND
The Law Book Company Ltd.
Sydney : Melbourne : Perth

CANADA AND U.S.A.
The Carswell Company Ltd.
Agincourt, Ontario

INDIA
N.M. Tripathi Private Ltd.
Bombay
and
Eastern Law House Private Ltd.
Calcutta and Delhi
M.P.P. House
Bangalore

ISRAEL
Steimatzky's Agency Ltd.
Jerusalem : Tel Aviv : Haifa

JUSTIFICATION AND EXCUSE
IN
THE CRIMINAL LAW

by

J. C. SMITH, C.B.E., Q.C., LL.D., F.B.A.

Honorary Bencher of Lincoln's Inn;
Honorary Fellow of Downing College, Cambridge;
Emeritus Professor of Law;
University of Nottingham.

Published under the auspices of

THE HAMLYN TRUST

LONDON
STEVENS & SONS
1989

Published in 1989
by Stevens & Sons Ltd.,
11 New Fetter Lane, London
Computerset by Promenade Graphics Ltd., Cheltenham
and printed in Scotland

British Library Cataloguing in Publication Data

Smith, John C.
Justification and excuse in the criminal
law.—(The Hamlyn lectures)
1. England. Criminal law
I. Title   II. Series
344.205

ISBN 0–420–47810–8
ISBN 0–420–47820–5 pbk

CONTENTS

THE HAMLYN LECTURES

THE HAMLYN TRUST

The Hamlyn Trust came into existence under the will of the late Miss Emma Warburton Hamlyn, of Torquay, who died in 1941 at the age of eighty. She came of an old and well-known Devon family. Her father, William Bussell Hamlyn, practised in Torquay as a solicitor for many years. She was a woman of strong character, intelligent and cultured, well versed in literature, music and art, and a lover of her country. She inherited a taste for law and studied the subject. She also travelled frequently to the Continent and about the Mediterranean, and gathered impressions of comparative jurisprudence and ethnology.

Miss Hamlyn bequeathed the residue of her estate in terms which were thought vague. The matter was taken to the Chancery Division of the High Court, which on November 29, 1948, approved a Scheme for the administration of the Trust. Paragraph 3 of the Scheme is as follows:

"The object of the charity is the furtherance by lectures or otherwise among the Common People of the United Kingdom of Great Britain and Northern Ireland of the knowledge of the Comparative Jurisprudence and Ethnology of the chief European countries including the United Kingdom, and the circumstances of the growth of such jurisprudence to the intent that the Common People of the United Kingdom may realise the privileges which in law and custom they enjoy in comparison with other European Peoples and realising and appreciating such privileges may recognise the responsibilities and obligations attaching to them."

The Trustees are to include the Vice-Chancellor of the University of Exeter and representatives of the Universities of London, Leeds, Glasgow, Belfast and Wales.

The Trustees under the Scheme number eight:

From the first the Trustees decided to organise courses of lectures of outstanding interest and quality by persons of eminence, under the auspices of co-operating Universities or other bodies, with a view to the lectures being made available in book form to a wide public.

The fortieth series of Hamlyn Lectures was delivered at the University of Newcastle upon Tyne in October 1988 by Professor J. C. Smith.

February 1989   DAVID M. WALKER

Chairman of the Trustees

Introduction

Defences at Common Law and by Statute

A person who does acts which exactly fit the definition of an offence is not necessarily liable to be convicted of that offence. The criminal law provides definitions, not only of offences but also of defences. It tells us the circumstances in which an act which would otherwise be a crime is justified or excused. Our criminal law is a somewhat haphazard mixture of common law and statute. The law relating to some offences is to be found only in the decisions of the courts—that is, in the common law—and not in any Act of Parliament. Murder, manslaughter and assault, for example are all still common law offences. Other offences, such as theft and most of its related offences, are defined by statute. It is the same with defences. Statute sometimes provides for defences applicable to crimes generally but more often for special defences to charges of a particular statutory offence. Most of the law relating to general defences—that is, defences which may be raised to a charge of any crime, or all but a few specified crimes—is still a matter of common law. Although some of this common law of defences has been thought by the Law

1

Commission to be ripe for statutory enactment, other parts of it are relatively undeveloped and one view is that, even if the criminal law is codified, these parts of the law should be left open for judicial development.

The courts have now renounced former claims to be entitled to develop the common law so as to create new crimes. It is true that generous interpretation of the terms of the definitions of existing offences, whether statutory or common law, may, in practice, significantly extend the reach of the criminal law from time to time; but that is as far as the courts may go in that direction. It may be said that if it is not the business of the courts to create new offences, it is not their business to create new defences either: innovation in the criminal law is for Parliament, not the judges. That opinion may well have been reinforced by our recent unhappy experiences in relation to the defence of duress. Duress is a general defence where the accused did the act which would otherwise be criminal only because of a threat of death or serious personal violence so great as to overbear the ordinary powers of human resistance. For centuries it was said that duress could not be a defence to a charge of murder. Then, in 1975 in *Lynch's case*,[1] the House of Lords decided that the defence could be available to a person charged with murder as an accessory. In the case of *Howe and Bannister* last year the House changed its mind and some of their Lordships were rather critical of their predecessors. Lord Hailsham said[2]:

" . . . the attempt made in *Lynch's case* to clear up this situation by judicial legislation has proved to be an excessive and perhaps improvident use of the undoubted power of the courts to create new law by creating precedents in individual cases."

[1] *D.P.P. for Northern Ireland* v. *Lynch* [1975] A.C. 653.
[2] [1987] A.C. 417 at p. 430.

Lord Bridge said[3]:

" . . . it is . . . by legislation alone, as opposed to judicial development, that the scope of the defence of duress can be defined with the degree of precision which, if it is to be available in murder at all, must surely be of critical importance."

Whatever the relative merits of the decision in *Lynch* and its reversal by *Howe*—a matter to which I shall return—it is certainly true that judicial decisions which make the law more lenient bring their own difficulties. The effect is retrospective in that the judicial decision declares that the common law was always as it is now declared to be, or that the correct interpretation of a statute has always been what it is now declared to be. So judges who quite properly directed juries according to the law prevailing at the time of the trial, *mis*directed them. If such a retrospectively wrong direction is a recent one it may still be possible to appeal against a resulting conviction but, if the time limit for appeal has run out, the only course open to a person convicted on a direction denying him a defence which we now know should have been open to him, is to petition the Home Secretary to exercise his power to refer the case to the Court of Appeal[4]—and that is something that the Home Secretary may be very reluctant to do, especially if large numbers of convicted persons may be involved. This consideration has not inhibited the courts in some important recent cases where they have been satisfied that earlier decisions were wrong and unduly favourable to the prosecution.

That great judge, Stephen J., the author of the draft Criminal Code of 1879, was firmly of the opinion that, while the power of the judges to create new crimes should certainly be taken away, it would be wrong to enact an exclusive

---

[3] At p. 437–438.
[4] *Pegg* [1988] Crim.L.R. 370 and commentary.

definition of circumstances of justification or excuse. To provide that in no other circumstances than those expressly stated should there be a defence, in his opinion[5]—

" . . . would be to run a risk, the extent of which it is difficult to estimate, of producing a conflict between the Code and the moral feelings of the public. Such a conflict is upon all possible grounds to be avoided. It would, if it occurred, do more to discredit codification than anything which could possibly happen and it might cause serious evils of another kind. Cases sometimes occur in which public opinion is at once violently excited and greatly divided, so that conduct is regarded as criminal or praiseworthy according to the sympathies of excited partisans. If the Code provided that nothing should amount to an excuse or justification which was not within the express words of the Code, it would, in such a case, be vain to allege that the conduct of the accused person was morally justifiable; that, but for the Code, it would have been legally justifiable; that every legal analogy was in its favour; and that the omission of an express provision about it was probably an oversight. I think such a result would be eminently unsatisfactory."

However carefully offences are defined, situations will occur from time to time of which all, or almost all, right-thinking people—the "Common People" to whom Miss Hamlyn wished these lectures to be addressed—would say that it would be right to break the letter of the law. If defences, as well as offences, have closed definitions, there is, in such a case, no escape from the conflict which Stephen feared: the law declares to be criminal conduct which the Common People think to be right. The consequences might be mitigated by administrative action—by exercising the

[5] *The Nineteenth Century*, January 1880, at p. 8, 153–154, more fully cited by Glanville Williams, [1978] Crim.L.R. 128.

discretion not to prosecute, by imposing no penalty, or a nominal penalty or by granting a pardon; but the conflict remains.

I will illustrate the unwisdom, as it seems to me, of an exclusive statement of justification or excuse by reference to the law of abortion and the famous case of *Bourne*[6] in 1938 when a surgeon of the greatest integrity and skill performed an operation of abortion on a 14-year-old girl who was pregnant as the result of a vicious rape. He certainly deliberately broke the letter of the law, section 58 of the Offences against the Person Act 1861; but he was acquitted by a jury who were directed by Macnaghten J. that it was a defence for the doctor to show that the act was done in good faith for the purpose only of preserving the life of the mother, although, at that time, there was no provision of such a defence in the statute. Since then Parliament has passed the Abortion Act 1967 which provides that a person is not guilty of an offence if he terminates a pregnancy in accordance with the conditions specified in section 1 of the Act. Section 5(2) provides:

"For the purposes of the law relating to abortion, anything done with intent to procure the miscarriage of a woman is unlawfully done unless authorised by section 1 of this Act."

This is evidently intended to abolish any such common law defence as was applied in *Bourne*. But suppose that a fully qualified doctor, who is not a registered medical practitioner and so cannot satisfy the conditions of the 1967 Act, finds that the immediate termination of a pregnancy is necessary in order to save the life of a mother who is in a remote place and beyond the help of any registered practitioner. He is in a position to perform the operation safely. Is it really the law that he must let the woman die, when he could save her by

---

[6] [1939] 1 K.B. 687, Central Criminal Court.

terminating the pregnancy?[7] If that is, as it appears to be, the effect of section 5(2), then we have an instance of the dreaded conflict. Of course, it is a very rare and unlikely case; but if the same principle were applied to offences generally, the effect could be far-reaching.

The Law Commission's Codification Team found Stephen's arguments persuasive.[8] The new draft Criminal Code which, it is hoped, will, in due course provide definitions of all offences known to the law, would leave in existence any power the courts now have "to determine the existence, extent or application of any rule of the common law" which justifies or excuses the doing of an otherwise criminal act, except insofar as the rule is inconsistent with any Act of Parliament. Under the Code common law offences would disappear but common law defences, to this extent, would be retained. Much of the law relating to justification and excuse is then less precisely defined than the elements of offences and seems likely to remain so. For this reason, among others, it is a part of the law of particular interest but one where it is more than usually difficult to know the limits of the law. It is also a matter of great public interest and concern as, I hope, will appear as I proceed with these lectures.

[7] See Smith & Hogan, *Criminal Law* (6th ed.), 372.
[8] Codification of the *Criminal Law: A Report to the Law Commission*, Law Com. No. 143, p. 116.

1. Justification or Excuse? Does it Matter?

The Distinction between Justification and Excuse

I turn to the question of what we mean by justification and excuse and whether there is any material distinction between them. The old common law made such a distinction in the law of homicide. Some homicides, like that done by the public hangman in carrying out the sentence of the court, were justifiable. The law actually required the hangman to kill. He was doing no more than his gruesome duty required. Other homicides, though not amounting to crimes, like killing by misadventure, were merely excusable. Such a killing, far from being required by the law was, no doubt, universally regarded as deplorable; but it was not a crime. Both justification and excuse resulted in acquittal on a charge of homicide but, if the homicide was only excusable, under the common law, the killer's goods were forfeited. In 1828 forfeiture was abolished and, since then, so far as the defendant is concerned, there has been no difference between the various defences to homicide or any other crime. Whether described as justification or excuse, the defence when successfully raised, results simply in a verdict of not guilty. Consequently

7

courts and text-writers ceased to draw any distinction between them and used the terms as if, for the purposes of criminal law, they were synonymous.

Recently, however, there has been a great revival of interest in a distinction between justification and excuse.[9] The matter has attracted the attention of leading academic writers, particularly in the United States. Notwithstanding the fact that justification and excuse both result simply in acquittal, it is said that the distinction has two, and, by some three, important consequences. It may, it is said, affect the liability of others in two ways.

1. Excusable conduct may be resisted by a person who is threatened by it; but justifiable conduct may not be resisted.
2. Excusable conduct may not lawfully be assisted by another but justifiable conduct may be.

Some, but not all, of the commentators would add:

3. Where the facts provide a justification for the defendant's conduct, he is justified even if he is unaware of those facts; and where the facts are capable only of excusing, the defendant is not excused unless he is aware of those facts.

If these arguments are well founded it is indeed important for us to make the distinction and to know which defences amount to justification and which merely to excuse.

Acts which are Unlawful in the Civil but not in the Criminal Law

In these lectures I am concerned principally with the criminal law but that is only part of the law and the civil law also has

[9] See especially G. Fletcher, *Rethinking Criminal Law*, Chap. 10, P. Robinson (1982) 82 Col. Law Rev. 199.

something to say about the matters I shall be discussing. Statutes, not infrequently, are expressed in general terms so that they are applicable in both the civil and the criminal courts. I will take as an example a provision to which I shall be making constant reference, section 3 of the Criminal Law Act 1967:

> "A person may use such force as is reasonable in the circumstances in the prevention of crime, or in effecting or assisting in the lawful arrest of offenders or suspected offenders or of persons unlawfully at large."

Although this provision appears in a Criminal Law Act, it is obviously not confined in its operation to the criminal law. It is expressed in quite general terms and it apparently authorises the use of reasonable force by any person against any other person or his property for one of the purposes mentioned. If a person—we will call him Dan—has used force in the circumstances described in section 3 against another person—we will call him Peter—and Peter sues Dan for damages in a civil court, it is clear that the section provides Dan with a defence to the action. Equally if Dan is prosecuted in a criminal court for assault, he must be acquitted. He has only done what Parliament has said he may do; and that cannot be a civil or a criminal wrong. But suppose that Dan was making a mistake about the circumstances. He thought Peter was making an unlawful attack on a third person and he intervened, as he thought, to prevent the commission of a crime when Peter, in fact, was behaving quite lawfully. Or he thought Peter was armed with a knife but in fact Peter was unarmed. In the actual circumstances it was not reasonable to use any force, or the degree of force in fact used. The words of the section are not satisfied. It authorises only such force as is reasonable in the circumstances. When Dan is sued in the civil court, the section is no answer: the force he used was not "reasonable in the circumstances." Dan may be held liable to pay damages to Peter for the injury he has inflicted. He has committed an unlawful act, a tort. But it does not necessarily follow that if he is prosecuted in a criminal court he will be found guilty. Criminal law generally requires proof of a guilty mind, *mens rea*, which is not required in a civil action. In 1983 the Criminal Division of the Court of Appeal decided in an important case, *Williams (Gladstone)*,[10] that in such a case as I have described the defendant is to be judged on the facts as he honestly believed them to be, whether reasonably or not. If the use of the force in question would have been reasonable had Peter in fact been making an attack on the third person or been armed with a knife, as Dan believed, then Dan has a defence to the criminal charge. He lacked the criminal mind which the criminal law requires. On the facts as he believes them to be, he *intended* to use only reasonable force—he *intended* to do only what the law says he may do.

In such a case it seems to me entirely appropriate to say of Dan's act that it is excused but not justified. It is not appropriate to say that it is justified because it is an unlawful act, a tort. But it is excused in the criminal law because the defendant, though possibly negligent, is not blameworthy in any sense recognised by the criminal law. The object of the civil law is to provide compensation for some injury which has occurred and to decide on which of two persons the loss should properly fall. The damage has been done, it has been done by the defendant and—we will assume—to a perfectly innocent person; and, as between that person and the defendant, certainly if he has been negligent, the defendant ought to bear the loss. But in the criminal court we are concerned not with compensation (except incidentally), but with punishment. The question is not how to allocate the burden of some existing loss but whether a new loss should be inflicted on the defendant—loss of his liberty or loss of his money by the imposition of a fine which goes to the state,

[10] [1987] 3 All E.R. 411.

not the victim. The question is whether the defendant deserves to be punished.

The distinction I have made between the liability of the defendant in the civil and criminal courts respectively is well recognised in the law; but it is not the basis of the distinction between justification and excuse which is made by some academic theorists. They pay no attention to the distinction between civil and criminal law but regard acts which they say are merely excused and not justified as "wrong" in some more general sense. It is also a less precise sense since it is nowhere prescribed in any statute, nor is it to be found in any case law. On the contrary, one of the constant complaints of the theorists is that the courts in modern times have paid no regard to the distinction between justification and excuse and have tended to use the terms as if they were synonymous— which is true—and that they have sometimes used them wrongly. The theory is that justified conduct is "good"—the actor has done something that society approves of—whereas merely excused conduct is "bad"—society disapproves of what has been done but accepts that the actor should not be punished.

There are some defences, especially those of a personal nature, where it is certainly appropriate to use the terms in this sense. No one would dream of saying that a nine-year old child who goes shoplifting or who deliberately stabs his playmate to death is "justified" in what he does; but the child is excused from criminal liability because the policy of the law is to fix the minimum age of criminal responsibility at 10 years. The same is true of a person who is insane within the M'Naghten Rules and who does acts which would be crimes in the case of a normal person. There are other cases where it is obviously equally appropriate to use the term, "justification." A gaoler who is charged with the crime of false imprisonment and who shows that he is carrying out the orders of the court establishes that he is justified in detaining the prisoner and not merely excused from criminal liability.

He is doing what society wants him to do and, in this case, has, through the proper authority, instructed him to do.

Between these two extremes there are, however, other cases where it is by no means clear how the defence should be characterised. It is debated whether certain acts done by way of self-defence or the defence of others are properly described as justified or excused. Whether the act is one which society wants to be done, or merely tolerates, is a question which is not easy to answer if society has not expressed its wishes in the form of legislation or judicial decision. Not unnaturally there is disagreement between the theorists. So far as the successful defendant is concerned, it matters not in the least whether the court, or anyone else, says that he is justified or merely excused; he is simply found not guilty in either event.

The Influence of Justification/Excuse Theory in Law Making

The distinction may, however be important when we consider how the law is formulated. Whether the defendant is successful in his defence may well depend on how the court, consciously or unconsciously, characterises it. If a court looks for actual justification and nothing less, the defence might fail whereas it would perhaps have succeeded if the court had merely looked for an excuse. The decision of the House of Lords in 1987 in the case of *Howe and Bannister*,[11] that duress can never be a defence to murder, has been much criticised on this ground. It is argued that their Lordships fell into error because their premise was that duress could never be a defence unless it justified the action of the defendant. As the killing of an innocent person was something of which they could never approve, duress could never be a defence to murder, however grave the threats involved. If they had

[11] [1987] A.C. 417.

considered that the question was whether the defendant deserved to be punished, or ought to be excused, they might have reached a different result. In the earlier case of *Lynch* v. *D.P.P. for Northern Ireland* Lord Edmund-Davies had cited[12] an observation of my own, made in the context of duress:

> "To allow a defence to crime is not to express approval of the action of the accused but only to declare that it does not merit condemnation and punishment."

A court may be more ready to acknowledge the existence of a defence if it is not seen to be giving approval to what has been done. The decision of the court may be different if it asks the question—

(1) "Is a person ever justified in killing an innocent person to save his own life?"—

instead of—

(2) "Does a person always deserve to be condemned as a murderer because he has killed an innocent person to save his own life?"

In my opinion, the second question is the right one for a criminal court. Its business is to decide what is forbidden by the criminal law and what is not; and it stops there. When the court decides that a defence applies it is no part of its duty to approve or disapprove of what has been done, though there may certainly be occasions when the court wishes to make it clear that it is doing no more than applying the criminal law and is not expressing approval of the acquitted defendant's action.

---

[12] [1975] A.C. 643 at p. 716, referring to "A Note on Duress," [1974] Crim.L.R. 349 at p. 352.

A Canadian View of Justification and Excuse

It might seem apparent that to require justification will always result in a narrower defence than merely to require a sufficient excuse. Yet, paradoxically, in one of the rare cases in which a court has given detailed consideration to the distinction between justification and excuse, the Supreme Court of Canada, on holding that a defence of necessity is recognised by Canadian criminal law, characterised the defence as an excuse rather than a justification and did so expressly for the purpose of confining the defence within narrower and acceptable limits. It is worth pausing to consider how this came about.

In *Perka et al.* v. *The Queen*[13] the appellants were drug smugglers who were employed to deliver by ship, *The Samarkanda*, a cargo of cannabis worth six or seven million dollars from a point in international waters off the coast of Colombia to a drop point in international waters 200 miles off the coast of Alaska. After they set sail the ship developed engine trouble and ran into very bad weather when 180 miles from the Canadian coastline. They sailed into a sheltered bay but ran aground on a rock. The captain, fearing that the ship was going to capsize, ordered the crew to off-load the cargo. So the cannabis was imported into Canada in order to save the ship from capsizing. The appellants were arrested and charged with importing cannabis into Canada and with possession of the drug for the purpose of drug trafficking. At their trial in British Columbia the smugglers raised the defence of necessity and were acquitted. On appeal by the prosecution the British Columbia Court of Appeal ordered a new trial, not because it questioned whether a defence of necessity existed in law but on a point of evidence—the trial judge had wrongly refused to allow the Crown to adduce

---

[13] (1984) 13 D.L.R. (4th) 1.

rebutting evidence as to the condition of the ship's engines, evidence which might have shown that, in the particular circumstances of this case, there was no necessity to bring the cannabis into Canada. The Supreme Court of Canada confirmed the decision of the Court of Appeal but gave full consideration to the defence of necessity. The judgment of the majority was delivered by Dickson J., soon to become Chief Justice of Canada. He observed that the defence of necessity is "capable of embracing two different and distinct notions," and he cited[14] the statement of another Canadian judge, MacDonald J.:

"Generally speaking, the defence of necessity covers all cases where non-compliance with law is excused by an emergency or justified by the pursuit of some greater good."

Dickson J. rejected the "greater good" basis for the defence. That theory envisages a person faced with a choice between two evils, at least one of which consists in a breach of the letter of the criminal law. If he chooses to break the letter of the criminal law, his action may be justified because the evil of that breach is outweighed by the evil which has been avoided. The theory, said Dickson J.[15]—

"involves a utilitarian balancing of the benefits of obeying the law as opposed to disobeying it, and when the balance is clearly in favour of disobeying, exculpates an actor who contravenes a criminal statute . . . in some circumstances, it is alleged, the values of society, indeed of the criminal law itself, are better promoted by disobeying a given statute than by observing it."

If this theory applies, the choice between the evils would have to be made, in the first place, by the person placed in

[14] At p. 12, citing *Salvador* (1981) 59 C.C.C. (2d) 521 at p. 542.
[15] See the discussion of *Buckoke* v. *Greater London Council* [1971] 1 Ch. 9, 655, below, p. 86.

the dilemma envisaged, but, clearly, the individual's choice could not be decisive. As Dickson J. said, affirming his own expression of opinion in an earlier case:

" . . . no system of positive law can recognise any principle which would entitle a person to violate the law because on his view the law conflicted with some higher social value."

It would ultimately be for a court to decide whether the defendant had made the right choice and whether the evil which he avoided, or intended to avoid, did indeed outweigh, and outweigh to a sufficient degree, the evil of breaking the law. This theory was unacceptable because—

"To . . . hold that ostensibly illegal acts can be validated on the basis of their expediency would import an undue subjectivity into the criminal law. It would invite the courts to second-guess the Legislature and to assess the relative merits of social policies underlying criminal prohibitions. Neither is a role which fits well with the judicial function."

So Dickson J. rejected the theory that necessity is a justification for breaking the letter of the law and held that it is properly regarded as an excuse, available only in situations of clear and imminent peril where the harm inflicted is less than the harm sought to be avoided. By treating necessity, not as a justification but as a mere excuse, he thought,

"The objectivity of the criminal law is preserved; such acts are still wrongful, but in the circumstances they are excusable. Praise is indeed not bestowed but pardon is. . . . "

The "emergency" theory confines the defence of necessity within narrower limits than the "greater good" theory, especially when the proviso is added that the excuse is available only when the harm inflicted by the breach of the letter of law must be less than the harm threatened by the emergency. Endless cases can be envisaged where, though there is no "emergency," it might plausibly be argued that greater good will come from breaking the law than observing it. Obviously the Canadian court was not deciding that an act may, at one and the same time, be justified but not excused, because that would not make sense. Anything which is justified must *a fortiori* be excused. The decision is that, in Canada, the "greater good" theory does *not*, in itself, provide a justification (or even an excuse) for breaking the letter of the criminal law.

In characterising the defence of necessity as an excuse rather than a justification, the Court was going against the great weight of that academic opinion which believes that all defences can be put into one category or the other and which regards the defence of duress as an excuse and that of necessity as a justification. I am not worried about the academic opinions—their authors can take care of themselves—but I do have great difficulty in accepting Dickson J.'s opinion that acts which are excused in law by necessity are still in some sense "wrongful"; and that opinion is difficult to reconcile with other passages in his judgment. For example—

" . . . the good Samaritan who commandeers a car and breaks the speed laws to rush an accident victim to hospital [is a person] whose actions we consider *rightful*, not wrongful."

In order not to mislead the Common People I should hasten to say that, in England, it is by no means clear that the good Samaritan would have a defence to a charge of speeding; but, if we assume with Dickson J. that there is a defence to that criminal charge, it can only be on the ground of necessity; and, given that the act is not a crime, I suspect that you and I, the Common People, would all agree that, if the driver is taking all reasonable care, the speeding envisaged is not wrongful in any other sense. Exceeding the speed limit *in itself* is "wrong" *only* because it is against the law—30 m.p.h. is an arbitrary figure selected by the legislator—and if the court decides that exceeding it is not wrong in law, it is not, in itself, wrong at all. I would like to be able to think that this very distinguished judge meant only to say that all that the success of a defence of necessity implies is that the defendant's conduct is, under the criminal law, excusable, leaving entirely open the question whether it is "right" or "wrong" in a moral or general sense. That would be an opinion I could entirely accept but, unfortunately, he does not leave room for that interpretation. Conduct excused by necessity is, he says, "always and by definition, wrongful." That is difficult to square with his example of the speeding good Samaritan and his opinion that his actions are rightful.

In *Perka's case* Dickson J. spoke for the majority but Wilson J.[16] delivered a separate judgment solely on the question of the conceptual basis of the defence of necessity. In his opinion, in some cases, necessity might afford not merely an excuse but also a justification for what would otherwise be a breach of the law. But those circumstances were very limited. There must be a conflict of legal duties and it must appear that the defendant made the right choice between them—that he chose the lesser of the two evils. He does not discuss Dickson J.'s good Samaritan but it would appear that, in Wilson J.'s opinion, the Samaritan would be justified only if he owed a duty to the victim of the accident, as he might if he was a relative or, possibly, if he was involved in the accident. But a mere passer-by (in English law, at least) owes no duty to stop and help those in trouble or in peril. As the whole point of the parable of the Good Samaritan, as I understand it, is that, unlike those who passed by on the other side, he was a stranger to the victim of the robbery whom he assisted, it would seem that the speeding driver envisaged is a person who owes no duty to the person assisted and therefore, according to Wilson J., could not be justified. Perhaps Wilson J. would regard him as excused, in which case the whole exercise of seeking to distinguish

[16] At p. 28.

between rightness and wrongness in a non-legal sense is some-what barren, since the verdict is exactly the same.

Consequences of a Distinction between Justification and Excuse

(i) *Resistance to Justifiable or Excusable Conduct*

It is said that merely excusable conduct may be resisted by a person who is threatened by it but that justifiable conduct may not. In cases where the defence falls very clearly into one or the other category the law, as I believe it to be, fits this theory very well. We have seen that the defence of infancy—being under the age of 10 years—is most appropriately des-cribed as an excuse and certainly not as a justification for doing an act which would be regarded as criminal if done by anyone of, or above, the age of criminal responsibility.

Suppose that a nine-year old child runs at me, holding out a long knife and shouting that he is going to kill me. If he were 10, he would appear, certainly when he gets close, to be guilty of attempted murder; but, because he is under the age of 10, he is incapable of committing crime. May I hit him with my walking stick as hard as is necessary in order to save myself from death or serious bodily harm? If I am unaware that he is under the age of 10, I certainly may do so because I am to be treated as if the facts were as I believed them to be, that is, as if I were defending myself against attempted mur-der. Suppose, however, that I know him to be only nine. I cannot now claim that my intention was to defend myself against a criminal attack or to prevent the commission of a crime because, on the facts known to me, the child's conduct is not criminal. I think this must be so, whether or not I am aware of the law which fixes the age of criminal responsibility at 10 years. Though there is surprising lack of authority on the point, it must surely be the law that I am entitled to use force, even deadly force, if that is necessary in order to preserve my own life against the infant aggressor. The child is excused from criminal responsibility, but not justified, in doing what he does and I may (it is submitted) resist with such force as is necessary and reasonable in the circumstances.

At the other extreme, consider the case of the gaoler who takes into custody a person sentence to imprisonment. It is a crime and a tort improperly to imprison another person but the gaoler's act is clearly justified, and not merely excused, because he is commanded by lawful authority to do it. It is equally clear that the prisoner is not justified or excused in resisting detention. He will commit offences if he does so. The law requires him to submit.

The Case of Stephen Waldorf

Between the extreme cases, however, there is an area in which it is by no means clear what the law is or what it ought to be. Consider the case of *Finch and Jardine* in 1982.[17] The defendants were police officers who shot and gravely injured an innocent man, Stephen Waldorf, in a public street. The officers believed that Waldorf was a dangerous escaped criminal, Martin. They knew that Martin had access to, and experience in the use of, firearms and that he was quite prepared to use them against anyone who got in his way. Waldorf had the misfortune to bear a striking resemblance to Martin and he was being driven in a mini-car with Martin's girl friend, whom the police had been tailing in the hope that she would lead them to Martin. The defendants were charged with attempted murder and wounding with intent to cause grievous bodily harm. Their defence was that they

---

[17] Central Criminal Court, October 12–19, 1982, unreported. The discussion following is based on the transcript of the shorthand notes of Geo. Walpole & Co., Official Shorthand Writers to the Central Criminal Court.

were acting in self defence or in defence of each other. In fact, of course, the officers were not being attacked. Waldorf was unarmed and had no intention of attacking the police or anyone else. It was conceded by the prosecution that everything that happened was the result of a genuine mistake by the officers. The judge, Croome-Johnson J., directed the jury that they "must look at the situation as it was at the time, and *as it presented itself to the two defendants.*" The defendants were to be judged on the facts as they believed them to be. The jury acquitted, as they were perfectly entitled to do on the evidence and the law. Waldorf was an entirely innocent man but the defendants committed no crime in wounding him.

Now the question in which I am particularly interested is whether a person in the situation of Mr. Waldorf is entitled to use force to defend himself. Of course, Waldorf had no opportunity to do so and the question did not arise. Let us therefore consider the case of one, X, the same in all material respects as that of Waldorf, except that X does have the opportunity to defend himself. He happens to be walking on the moors with the criminal's girl-friend and to be carrying a shotgun for the lawful purpose of shooting grouse. When he sees the police guns raised against him, may he fire first if this is the only way in which he can save himself from serious injury? It is necessary to make a distinction.

(a) Resister Unaware of Circumstances Justifying or Excusing Aggressor

Take first the case where X is quite reasonably unaware that his attackers are acting lawfully. He believes that he is the victim, not of a lawful, but of a criminal attack. The police—like the officers in Waldorf's case—are not in uniform but are wearing anoraks and there is nothing to tell him that he is dealing with police officers or that his assailants believe they are tackling a dangerous, armed criminal. He is then entitled to be treated as if the facts were as he honestly supposed them to be—and he believes that he is being attacked by a gang of armed thugs. If he would have been acting lawfully in shooting at the armed thugs he thought they were, then he commits no offence although they are in fact police officers, also acting lawfully and in the execution of their duty. Nor does it make any difference, it seems to me, whether the conduct of the officers is properly described as justified rather than excused. Even a justifiable attack may surely be resisted where the resister is unaware of the circumstances justifying his attacker's conduct. The police are not committing any offence but neither is X. It is a gun-battle without crime or criminal.

(b) Resister Aware of Circumstances Justifying or Excusing Aggressor

Suppose next that X is aware that his attackers are acting lawfully. To be more exact, he is aware of the circumstances which make the officers' act lawful for it is his knowledge of the relevant facts, not his knowledge of the law, which is material. X has been listening to his transistor radio. He has heard that armed police officers are searching the moor where he is walking, looking for the criminal. As they close in on him, X realises that they have mistaken him for that dangerous gunman. He finds himself looking into the muzzle of a gun and, believing that he is about to be shot, pulls the trigger of his shotgun and wounds or kills a police officer. He knows that he is shooting a police officer. He knows that the officer is hunting a dangerous criminal and believes that he, X, is that criminal. But he is also aware that he is not the criminal, that he has done nothing wrong and that his own life is in immediate danger, from which he can escape only by firing his gun. Has he a defence to a charge of unlawful wounding or murder?

Today this is no mere academic problem but a situation which is all too likely to arise in conditions of violent crime and, especially, terrorism such as that prevailing in Northern

Ireland. It appears probable that the Court of Appeal in Northern Ireland would say that X has no defence. In the case of *Browne*[18] in 1973 the appellant's counsel argued—

" . . . even where the police . . . are acting lawfully . . . the person being arrested may be justified in defending himself if the police are, according to the true facts (as opposed to those which they reasonably believe to be true) acting unjustifiably or unwarrantably."

That seems to be just the case I have put. The Court found that, on the facts, it was not necessary to decide the question but, *obiter*, they rejected counsel's argument. Lord Lowry C.J. said:

"We consider this proposition to be unsound and are of the opinion that the law throws, without any such refined reservations, a protecting mantle over persons preventing or assisting in preventing crime or making or assisting in making arrests."

It is probably true to say that an innocent person who is wrongly but reasonably suspected of having committed an arrestable offence must submit to arrest. In *Fennell*[19] the English Court of Appeal assumed without deciding that a father might lawfully use reasonable force to free his son from *unlawful* arrest by the police; but he acted at his peril and, if the arrest proved to be lawful—because, *e.g.* the police suspected reasonably, even if wrongly, that the son had committed an arrestable offence—then he was guilty of an assault on the police in the execution of their duty. But it is one thing to say that a person must submit to arrest. It is quite another to say that he must submit to the infliction of

---

[18] [1973] N.I. 96 at pp. 109–110.
[19] [1971] 1 Q.B. 428.

personal injury or even death. In *Fennell*[20] the Court said, *obiter*, that the father would have been acting lawfully if, under a genuine mistake of fact, he believed that his son was in imminent danger of injury and he had used reasonable force to prevent that. This dictum may have been intended to apply only to the case where the mistake led the father to believe that the police were acting unlawfully. In that case, it does not really assist us to solve the problem of whether X, in my hypothetical case, would commit an offence.

Some legal theorists would say that the answer turns on whether the aggressive but lawful conduct of the police was justified or merely excused. If that conduct was justified, then X was not entitled to resist and he is guilty. If it was merely excused, he was entitled to resist and, if he used no more than reasonable force, he is not guilty. And, as the officers were making a mistake and threatening an innocent man, they were only excused, not justified, so the defendant, X, does have an answer to the charge. These are, no doubt, "refined reservations" of a kind that the Northern Irish court was unwilling to entertain; but, with great respect, I would submit that, whatever the merits of the reasoning, the theorists have at least reached the better conclusion. But the justification/excuse theory cannot explain why (if it be the case) the wrongly but reasonably suspected person must submit to arrest but need not submit to the use of reasonable but dangerous force to make that arrest. The arrest, and the use of reasonable force to effect it, are both authorised by statute in terms which are indistinguishable in substance. Each is an act that Parliament has said the arrester *may* do.

I would put it simply on this ground: that a man who is otherwise innocent should not be held guilty of unlawful wounding or even murder if he did the act of wounding or killing only because it was, or appeared to him to be, necessary in order to save himself from death or serious bodily

---

[20] [1971] 1 Q.B. 428 at p. 431.

harm. Of course, it is true that, in such a case, he is wounding or killing an innocent person to save himself. The police officer is acting lawfully in pursuance of his reasonable suspicion that he is dealing with a dangerous offender and that his own life is in danger, even though it turns out that he is mistaken. He is doing his duty and perhaps doing it heroically. And, maybe, our defendant knows this. Perhaps a person with very high standards of morality and heroism would submit to being shot rather than take the life of his innocent aggressor. We shall notice later that in *Howe and Bannister* some judges thought that the criminal law should, and indeed, in the law relating to duress, does, enforce such high standards; but that is point of view which I venture to question.

The academic theorists' opinion that X's liability to conviction depends on whether the conduct of the police is justified or merely excused certainly raises issues of some complexity. It becomes necessary to distinguish between force used in making an arrest and force used in self defence. The former is regulated by statutes, the latter by the common law. Parliament has provided by section 24 of the Police and Criminal Evidence Act 1984 that, where an arrestable offence has been committed, any person *may arrest* without a warrant, not only anyone who is guilty of the arrestable offence, but also anyone whom he has reasonable grounds for suspecting to be guilty of it; and, by section 3 of the Criminal Law Act 1967, that he *may use such force* as is reasonable in the circumstances in the lawful arrest, not only of offenders, but also of suspected offenders. It is true that the suspicions of the officers are mistaken but, even so, if the force they use is no greater than is, in the circumstances as they believe them to be, reasonable for the purpose of arresting the supposed offender, they are doing no more than Parliament has declared they may do. The same word, "may," applies whether the person being arrested is an actual offender or merely a suspected offender, who may turn out to be quite innocent. If the suspicion is reasonable and the force used is reasonable for making an arrest, the police are not even committing any civil wrong. It is difficult to see that their conduct can be described in any sense as "wrong," or that they have done something that "society" does not want them to do. Parliament has said that anyone, police officer or not, may do these acts because we want persons who are reasonably suspected of having committed serious offences to be arrested and we want the arrester to be able to use reasonable force if that is necessary.

That is the position regarding the use of force to make an arrest. But it will rarely, if ever, be permissible to kill or to wound simply in order to make an arrest. In *Finch and Jardine* it was the prosecution who alleged that the two officers fired in order to arrest the man they believed to be Martin and that their doing so amounted to attempted murder and unlawful wounding. The defendants denied that they were shooting in order to make an arrest. They said they were acting in self-defence and fired only because they thought that the man was about to shoot them. The judge agreed with this view of the law and he told the jury that, if Finch was trying to make a single-handed arrest of Martin, and not acting in self-defence, they should convict. Even in the case of such a very dangerous criminal as Martin, it was not reasonable to shoot at him simply in order to arrest him.

If it is necessary to go into the question of justification or excuse in our hypothetical case of X we must ask, was X resisting the justifiable use of force to make an arrest? Or was he resisting the lawful use by the officers of force in self-defence? If the police officer had fired before he thought he was under attack, he would not have been acting in pursuance of his statutory authority to use force in making an arrest because that would have been an excessive use of force. If he was acting lawfully at all, it was because he was acting in self-defence. So, X was not resisting an act done in pursuance of the statutory authority but an act done in self-defence. Self-defence is a matter of common law. No statute yet declares that a person *may* do acts which he reasonably but mistakenly believes to be necessary by way of self-defence. One view is that such acts are only excused; and this, in my opinion, leads to the right result: X is not guilty; but that, in my view, should be the answer whether the police conduct is rightly described as justified or excused. The liability of the resister should depend on what it is reasonable to expect of him.

(ii) *Assisting a Person with a Defence*

I turn now to the second consequence that is said to follow from the distinction between justification and excuse—that justifiable conduct may be an assisted by another but merely excusable conduct may not. Once again the theory works very well in extreme cases.

Justifiable conduct such as that of the gaoler in detaining the properly sentenced offender may be assisted with impunity by others. Where a constable has reasonable grounds for suspecting that an arrestable offence has been committed, he may arrest without a warrant anyone whom he has reasonable grounds for suspecting to be guilty of the offence. The arrest is lawful, even if it turns out that the no such offence was committed. A person other than a constable who makes an arrest in such circumstances has made an unlawful arrest if the offence was not committed. If, however, that person was not making the arrest himself but was assisting a constable in doing so, it is thought that he would do no wrong because the arrest by the constable which he is assisting is a lawful one.

On the other hand, it follows from the personal nature of defences such as infancy or insanity that only the child or the insane person can rely on them. You will recall my nine-year old attacker. An adult person who gave the nine-year old the knife and incited him to kill me would be guilty of attempted murder through the innocent agency of the child. He could

not shelter behind the child's defence.[21] But in cases other
than these extreme examples, the distinction seems either
unhelpful or pernicious. Consider a bystander who, in the
circumstances of Waldorf's case, comes to the assistance of
the police. A decision that the police were not justified but
merely excused and therefore that the bystander is liable for
the wounding done by the police would be outrageous. His
liability should depend on whether his intervention was justified or excused on the facts which he believed to exist.

(iii) *Unknown Circumstances of Justification or Excuse*

Thirdly it is said that circumstances which justify conduct are
a defence whether or not the defendant knows that they
exist; but that circumstances which are capable only of excusing do not excuse unless the defendant is aware of them.

In the case of some defences awareness is obviously
required because the whole essence of the defence is the
effect of the circumstances on the defendant's mind. Let me
take a rather far-fetched example—such examples are often
the most vivid way of illustrating some legal principle or

---

[21] The problem is more difficult where the adult assists without inciting. He
leaves the knife where the child will find it in the well-founded expec-
tation that he will use it to attack me. It is impossible to describe the child
as the adult's agent. One who intentionally assists another to commit an
offence is generally liable as an aider and abettor of that offence; but
there is a difficulty here for the child, *ex hypothesi*, has committed no
offence. There are cases (*Bourne* (1952) 36 Cr.App.R. 125, C.C.A.;
Cogan and Leake [1976] Q.B. 217) which hold that, where the *actus reus*
(the external facts) of an offence has been committed by a person who
cannot be convicted because he lacks the requisite mental state, or
because he has a defence, one who has aided and abetted him with a
guilty mind and without any defence may be convicted. But it is by no
means clear that the act of the child can be considered an *actus reus*; so
the excuse of the child may also excuse the adult.

problem. I am standing in front of Fred's house with a brick in my hand. I have a grudge against Fred and I am contemplating throwing the brick through his window. By a remarkable coincidence, George comes up behind me with a gun in his hand. He says, "Throw that brick through Fred's window or I'll blow your brains out." But I am hard of hearing. I am quite unaware that George is there, let alone that he is threatening me. I finally make up my mind to avenge my grudge against Fred and throw the brick through the window. I am duly charged with causing criminal damage. Duress is a defence to a charge of causing criminal damage and, if I had heard the threat and thrown the brick in consequence of it, I would certainly have had a good defence to the charge. But, as I did not hear it, it is plain that duress is not a defence. The courts have constantly insisted that the essence of duress is that the defendant's will is "overborne" by the threat. The elements of the defence include not only the external facts but the defendant's knowledge of them. This accords with academic theories because duress is said to be an excuse and not a justification. Where, however, the defence amounts to a justification, it is argued by some that the external facts are an answer to the charge even if the defendant is unaware of them. Because the facts in themselves justify his conduct, he has done nothing wrong and cannot be convicted of the crime, whatever his state of mind.

A useful example, though again a highly improbable one, is that of the public hangman who decides to hang the condemned man without waiting for any authorisation to do so. That looks like murder, but it turns out that, unknown to the hangman, authority had been given just before he did the deed. It is argued that this is not murder because he has only done what the law authorises him, indeed, requires him, to do. As the lawyers put it, there is no *actus reus*—whatever his state of mind, he has done nothing wrong. If we accept that then the principle might be applied to other more plausible cases. Much discussion has centred around the old case of

Dadson,[22] decided in 1850. The defendant was a constable
employed to watch a copse from which wood had been
stolen. He carried a loaded gun. X emerged from the copse,
carrying wood which he had stolen. He ignored Dadson's
calls to stop and ran away. Dadson, having no other means of
stopping him, fired and wounded him in the leg. He was convicted of unlawfully shooting at X with intent to cause him
grievous bodily harm. It was assumed in that case that it was
in those days lawful to wound an escaping felon in order to
arrest him. Dadson's defence was that he was not acting
unlawfully because X was an escaping felon. But, under section 39 of the Larceny Act 1827, stealing growing wood was
not a felony unless the thief had two previous convictions for
the same offence. In fact, X had repeatedly been convicted
of stealing wood so he was a felon; but Dadson did not know
this. At the trial, Erle J. told the jury that the alleged felony,
being unknown to the prisoner, constituted no justification.
Dadson was convicted and, on a case reserved, the judges
thought that the conviction was right.

Professor Glanville Williams[23] has for many years maintained that this decision was wrong. If it were right, he
argues, it would follow that—

"a British soldier who kills an enemy in action, believing
himself to be killing his own drill-sergeant, is guilty of murder"

—a conclusion which he declares to be preposterous. It
would be preposterous, but I suggest that it is a materially
different case. Murder has for centuries been defined as the
killing of a person "under the Queen's peace." An enemy
soldier making war against the Queen is not under the

---

[22] (1850) 4 Cox C.C. 358.
[23] *The Criminal Law, the General Part*, (1st ed., 1953), 22, (2nd ed., 1961),
p. 22.

Queen's peace so an element in the definition of the crime of murder is missing. Dadson, on the other hand undoubtedly shot at X with intent to cause him grievous bodily harm. But, it may be replied, the definition of the offence with which he was charged includes the word, "unlawfully," and Dadson did not cause the harm "unlawfully" because X was in fact an escaping felon and therefore it was lawful to shoot him. In my opinion, that answer begs the question. The question is whether unknown circumstances of justification justify shooting or not. If they do, then certainly Dadson's action was not unlawful; but, if they do not, then it was unlawful. The soldier's case is different because there an element of the offence—"a human being under the Queen's peace"—is certainly missing so there could be no question of convicting him of murder.

In *Dadson*, all the elements of the definition of the offence, subject to any meaning to be given to the word, "unlawfully," were present. If the use of the word, "unlawfully," in the definition of an offence has any effect at all, it is to make it clear that general defences to crime apply to that offence; so the remaining question was whether the elements of a defence were present. The word "unlawfully" says nothing at all about the nature of the general defences. Some defences, like duress, as has been observed, necessarily involve a mental element on the part of the defendant. The question which the judges had to decide in *Dadson* was whether the defence on which Dadson relied requires such a mental element—*i.e.* knowledge of the facts which justify the arrest and the use of force to effect it. This, I suggest, is a matter of policy. There is no rule of logic which requires it to be answered one way or the other. The answer given by the court in *Dadson* was, in my opinion, a perfectly reasonable one. On the facts known to the defendant, there was no justification or excuse for firing the gun and there is much to be said for a rule prohibiting the use of such force unless the user is aware of facts which justify or excuse it. Whether the justifying facts exist or not is a matter of pure chance and the actor's conduct is no better because it turns out that they do.

Whether knowledge of the facts should be required to found a defence, be it justification or excuse, is, I suggest, a matter of policy. The nine-year old delinquent who has appeared from time to time in this lecture cannot properly be said to be justified in doing acts that would be crimes if he were aged 10. He is only excused. But suppose he thinks he is 10. Is he then to be convicted of crime because he is unaware of the circumstance of excuse—that is, that he is aged only nine? Of course he may not be convicted. It is the policy of the law that children under 10 years of age shall not be convicted of crime and the child's belief clearly cannot be allowed to defeat that policy.

Professor Williams has, however, said,[24] with some justification, that, "on one notable occasion" the legislature has accepted his view. The occasion was the enactment of the Criminal Law Act 1967, section 2:

"(2) Any person may arrest without warrant anyone who is, or whom he, with reasonable cause, suspects to be, in the act of committing an arrestable offence.

(3) Where an arrestable offence has been committed, any person may arrest without warrant anyone who is, or whom he, with reasonable cause, suspects to be guilty of the offence . . .

(5) A constable may arrest without warrant any person who is, or whom he, with reasonable cause, suspects to be, about to commit an arrestable offence."

Professor Williams observes: "This means that a person who *is* committing or *is* guilty of the offence can be arrested even though the arrester has no reasonable cause for suspect-

---

[24] *Textbook of Criminal Law* (1st ed., 1978), p. 458.

ing him." Section 2 of the 1967 Act has now been repealed and the provisions cited are replaced by the Police and Criminal Evidence Act 1984, section 24(4), (5) and (7), which is even more explicit:

> "(4) Any person may arrest without a warrant—
>   (a) anyone who is in the act of committing an arrestable offence;
>   (b) anyone whom he has reasonable grounds for suspecting to be committing such an offence.
> (5) Where an arrestable offence has been committed, any person may arrest without a warrant—
>   (a) anyone who is guilty of the offence;
>   (b) anyone whom he has reasonable grounds for suspecting to be guilty of it . . .
> (7) A constable may arrest without a warrant—
>   (a) anyone who is about to commit an arrestable offence;
>   (b) anyone whom he has reasonable grounds for suspecting to be about to commit an arrestable offence."

These provisions authorise arrest and section 3 of the Criminal Law Act 1967, I would remind you, authorises the use of force for, among other things, effecting a lawful arrest:

> "(1) A person may use such force as is reasonable in the circumstances in the prevention of crime, or in effecting or assisting in the lawful arrest of offenders or suspected offenders or of persons unlawfully at large."

All this does not however mean that a person can justify the use of force against another merely by showing that the other was in the act of committing, or had committed, an arrestable offence. The person using force must show at least that he intended to effect an arrest. Section 2 justifies arrest and nothing more; and section 3 of the 1967 justifies the use of force only to carry out one of the specified lawful purposes. If the defendant uses force while purporting to act in self-defence, and not in order to make an arrest, he cannot justify his action by reference to section 24 and section 3. This appears from the Northern Irish case of *Thain*.[25]

The Case of Private Thain

Private Thain, a soldier in the light infantry, shot and killed a young man, Reilly, whom he was pursuing after Reilly had committed an assault on another member of the patrol to which Thain belonged. Reilly was unarmed but Thain said he fired in self-defence because Reilly, as he ran, looked back at him and he thought Reilly was reaching for a pistol and was going to use it. After a very careful review of the evidence, both the trial judge and the Court of Appeal in Northern Ireland disbelieved Thain's story. They accepted that he was to be judged on the facts as he believed them to be, but they were satisfied beyond reasonable doubt that he did not believe that he was about to be shot at. So self-defence failed. But Thain's counsel, citing Professor Glanville Williams's Textbook,[26] relied on what is there described as "the Unknown Necessity." Counsel appears to have argued that the force used by Thain was necessary and reasonable—or, at least that a court or jury might have found it to be necessary and reasonable—for the purpose of making an arrest. We must assume for this purpose (though this is contrary to the actual facts), first, that Reilly had been party to the shooting or stabbing of a soldier and, second, that, in those circumstances, it would have been lawful to use deadly force in order to arrest him. But, even making those assumptions, Thain had no defence. He himself stated that, when he was pursuing Reilly, he had decided that, if Reilly did not stop, he would let him get away; that he had decided not to

[25] (1985) Northern Ireland Law Reports Bulletin, 31 at pp. 66, 73–74.
[26] 1st ed., p. 457.

shoot, and did not shoot, to make an arrest; that he shot only in self defence. That being so, it was no answer to the charge of murder that he would have been justified in shooting to make an arrest. The Northern Irish Court of Appeal said:

> "We hold that the learned trial judge was correct when he held that an accused, whose evidence that he had decided not to fire to effect an arrest has been accepted as true, cannot rely on the defence that the firing was force used 'in effecting an arrest.' "

This is surely right in principle. So even where a person relies on (4)(*a*), (5)(*a*) or (7)(*a*) of section 24 of the Police and Criminal Evidence Act he has to give evidence of something more than the fact stated in the paragraph. He must show that he was acting for the purpose of effecting an arrest and not for some other purpose.

A purpose of arresting is a necessary condition of reliance on section 24 and, it is submitted, that purpose must, in common sense, be to arrest for the particular arrestable offence which is being, or has been, or is about to be committed. Suppose that Dan arrests Peter because Peter has called him a liar. Of course, Dan has no right to do that. It looks a plain case of an unlawful arrest. But wait a moment. It turns out that Peter has been shoplifting that morning. "Where an arrestable offence has been committed, any person may arrest without a warrant . . . anyone who is guilty of the offence:" section 24(5)(*a*). An arrestable offence has been committed and Peter is guilty of it. Literally, the words of the section are satisfied. But if Peter's unknown shoplifting justifies his arrest by Dan, so too must the fact that Peter committed bigamy five years ago—which is utterly preposterous. But it is not common sense alone which compels the conclusion that the arrest must be related to the particular arrestable offence which has in fact been committed. By section 28(3) of the Police and Criminal Evidence Act, enacting a principle of the common law—

"no arrest is lawful unless the person arrested is informed of the ground for the arrest at the time of, or as soon as practicable after, the arrest."

If Dan informs Peter that he has arrested him on the ground that Peter called him a liar, the arrest is surely unlawful, however many arrestable offences Peter may in fact have committed. " . . . the ground for the arrest" cannot mean some completely spurious ground. It must mean a ground set out in section 24 or some other provision which authorises arrest. If then an arrest is made on some ground which is insufficient in law of a person who has in fact committed an arrestable offence, it is clearly an unlawful arrest when that insufficient ground is declared. But is it to be said that it only becomes unlawful on that point? That would be absurd. An action done for a bad reason does not become worse when that reason is disclosed. The arrest must surely be unlawful from the start. So, for an arrest to be lawful, the arrester must be in a position from the start to declare as soon as practicable a valid ground of arrest, related to the offence which in fact is being, or has been, or is about to be committed. I do not mean, of course, that the arrester must know the correct legal name or description of the offence, but that he must know the facts which constitute it.[27]

The conclusion is that the difference in effect between the three paragraphs (*a*) of section 24 on the one hand, and the three paragraphs (*b*) of that section, on the other, is less than is sometimes supposed. The paragraphs (*a*) do not justify arrest simply because certain facts exist. Arrest is lawful under the (*a*) paragraphs only if the arrester believes, or at least suspects, that the person being arrested is (i) committing, or (ii) guilty of, or (iii) about to commit, the arrestable offence (or an arrestable offence closely related to it) that he is in fact committing, or guilty of, or about to commit. Unless

---

[27] *cf. Chapman* v. *D.P.P.* [1988] Crim.L.R. 843, C.A.

he has the belief or suspicion described, he cannot satisfy the conditions of section 28(3), requiring disclosure of the ground for the arrest and, if those conditions are unfulfilled, the arrest is unlawful.

The only difference in the mental state required for arrest under the paragraphs (*a*) and (*b*) respectively is that under the paragraphs (*a*) the arrester need have no reasonable grounds for his suspicion or belief. Even if his suspicion or belief is unreasonable, the arrest is lawful because the arrested person is in fact committing, or guilty of, or about to commit, the arrestable offence for which he is being arrested.[28] As Professor Williams says,[29] it justifies an arrest "on hunch" that the suspect is guilty of the particular offence; but that is as far as it goes.

In the light of this analysis, it appears that section 24(5)(*a*) would have been of no help to Dadson had it been in force at the time of his case. Suppose that Dadson had caught up with X and arrested him saying, "I arrest you on the ground that you have stolen wood from the copse." That was not a valid ground for arrest. The offence stated was not a felony but an offence punishable only on summary conviction by a fine of £5 and there was no power to arrest the offender. Dadson could state no valid ground for arrest so as to satisfy the conditions of section 28(3) for he knew of none. For the reasons given above, it is submitted that the arrest would have been unlawful from the start; and, of course, it follows that the wounding would also have been unlawful.

The nature of the offences involved in *Dadson* was peculiar in that the offence assumed an aggravated character if

---

[28] A reasonable suspicion that an arrestable offence has been committed "is the source from which all a constable's powers of arrest flow . . . ," *per* Bingham L.J. in *Chapman* v. *D.P.P.*, footnote 27, above. But his Lordship was not concerned with, and probably did not have in mind, a case where it is proved that the arrestable offence has in fact been committed.

[29] *Textbook of Criminal Law* (2nd ed., 1983) pp. 489–490; 2 *Legal Studies*, 244–247.

the offender had previous convictions. Offences of this type have disappeared from the law but there are other circumstances which are indistinguishable in principle. Suppose that Dan sees Peter taking his bicycle. He believes that Peter is taking his bicycle without permission in order to go for a ride on it, as he has done on several occasions in the past. If Dan arrests Peter and informs him that he is arrested for taking the bike without permission, this is an unlawful arrest. Taking a pedal cycle without the consent of the owner is an offence punishable on summary conviction under the Theft Act 1968, section 12(5), but it is not an arrestable offence. Suppose, further that, on this occasion, Peter was taking the bike, not merely to go for a ride, but to sell it and deprive Dan permanently of it. He was stealing the bike and that is an arrestable offence. Section 24(4)(*a*) is literally satisfied but section 28(3) is not for, though a ground for arrest has been stated, it is not a valid ground. If Dan had suspected Peter of stealing the bike, even without reasonable grounds, and declared that to be the ground of arrest, then his action would have been lawful under paragraph (*a*), though not under paragraph (*b*), of section 24(4). It would not be difficult to construct many other similar examples.

The Dadson Principle and Private Defence

The statutory modification of the *Dadson* principle that we have been considering applies only to powers of arrest and force used in making a lawful arrest. It leaves open the question whether that principle applies to other justifications or excuses for the use of force, especially self-defence or the defence of others, conveniently called "private defence." Let me introduce the problem by another of my far-fetched examples.

Peter is now a notorious practical joker. One day, he enters the office of his colleague, Dan, points at Dan what Dan supposes to be a toy pistol and says, "You have got to die." Dan, who has been irritated beyond endurance by

Peter's merry japes, responds by throwing his heavy inkstand which hits Peter on the head and kills him. Full of remorse, Dan phones the police and tells them that he has killed a man simply for playing a practical joke on him. But when the police examine the pistol they find that it is a real one and loaded. Further, they find a note in Peter's room, stating that he is going to kill Dan, whom he detests, and then commit suicide. If Dan had not thrown the inkstand, it appears likely that he would have been shot dead. If Dan is charged with murder or manslaughter, can he successfully claim that he was acting in self-defence? Can he rely on unknown circumstances of justification or excuse? Though the matter is not mentioned in their report, the Criminal Law Revision Committee (as Professor Williams has revealed,[30] and as I can confirm) debated at some length whether the *Dadson* principle should apply to private defence. They concluded, Professor Williams dissenting, that it should. Circumstances unknown to the defendant should be ignored. Their recommendation[31] was that—

"The common law of self-defence should be replaced by a statutory defence providing that a person may use such force as is reasonable in the circumstances as he believes them to be in the defence of himself or any other person, or in the defence of his property or that of any other person."

The principle is stated exclusively in terms of the defendant's belief. It does not, on its face, afford a defence in a case where the defendant was unaware of existing circumstances which, if he knew of them, would justify or excuse his use of force. The Committee thought that, insofar as their proposal did not require reasonable grounds for the defendant's

---

[30] "Offences and Defences," 2 *Legal Studies* 233 at p. 251.
[31] Fourteenth Report, *Offences against the Person*, Cmnd. 7844 (1980), para. 287.

belief, they were recommending a change in the law. Subsequently, however, in a series of cases beginning with *Williams (Gladstone)*[32] it has been held that the recommendation represents the existing law. The courts in these cases have not adverted to the *Dadson* issue but it seems probable that the present law is that private defence is an answer to the charge only if the defendant *intended* to act in defence of himself or another *and* was aware of the circumstances which entitled him to do so. The defence would not be available to Dan, whether it is properly described as a justification or an excuse.

When the Codification Team came to consider the issue, they thought that there was much to be said in favour of the *Dadson* principle but, under their terms of reference, it was clearly not possible to provide for its application in relation to force used in making an arrest. To do so would have been inconsistent with section 2 of the Criminal Law Act 1967 and with the clause in the Police and Criminal Evidence Bill, then before Parliament, which become section 24 of the 1984 Act—even on the assumption that these provisions have the limited effect attributed to them above. The Team ascertained that the Home Office was aware of the effect of section 2, as they interpreted it,[33] and that they intended it to be reiterated in the Bill. The Act was passed before the publication of the Codification report and it would clearly have been futile to make a recommendation contradicting so recent a decision of Parliament, expressed in such emphatic terms as section 24. To accept the will of Parliament and at the same time to follow the recommendation of the Committee would have required the exclusion of the *Dadson*

---

[32] (1984) 78 Cr.App.R. 276; *Jackson* [1985] R.T.R. 257; *Asbury* [1986] Crim.L.R. 258; *Beckford* v. *R.* [1988] A.C. 130 (P.C.).

[33] At that time the team did not consider whether the effect of the provisions might be limited as suggested above and it should not be assumed that members of the team, other than the writer, would necessarily agree with that interpretation.

principle with respect to force used in making an arrest and the application of the principle with respect to force used in private defence. The team concluded that such a distinction was impracticable.[34]

> "A person making an arrest is frequently acting in the prevention of crime; and a person acting in the prevention of crime is also frequently acting in self-defence or the defence of others. To have different rules according to the purpose of the user of the force when the purposes may be indistinguishable would defeat one of the primary objects of codification, namely the enactment of a consistent and coherent body of law."

The team therefore concluded that it was necessary to exclude the *Dadson* principle from the whole range of defences justifying or excusing the use of force in the arrest of offenders, prevention of crime and private defence. It is probable that this provision, if enacted, would change the law of private defence as now stated in *Williams (Gladstone)*. Some, including, presumably, all the members of the Criminal Law Revision Committee who signed the Fourteenth Report, except Professor Williams, would consider this a change for the worse. For those of that opinion, the justification, if any, must be that it is better to have a consistent second-best rule than one which would sometimes produce the "best" result and sometimes the "second-best," with a confusing and uncertain overlap between the two.

Dadson and Attempts to Commit Crime

Professor Williams, always ahead of the field, anticipated the modern debate about justification and excuse in his early discussion of Dadson's case.[35] He distinguished the situation where "the law wishes to promote a consequence" from that

---

[34] Law Com. No. 143, at pp. 122–123.
[35] *The Criminal Law, The General Part*, (2nd ed., 1961) pp. 25–26.

where it "merely refrains from imposing a prohibition." It was only in the former case that he thought that unknown facts should be a defence—in effect, that unknown circumstances of justification are an answer to the charge but circumstances which would merely excuse if they were known, do not excuse if they are unknown. *Dadson* fell into the former category because "the law wishes to promote" the arrest of felons, or their modern equivalent. Recognising the difficulty of making this distinction, it was with some hesitation that he at first put self-defence into the "excuse" category—a case where the law merely refrains from imposing a prohibition. In the case of excuses, he then thought that the *Dadson* principle was acceptable: the person who killed or wounded should not be able to rely on self-defence if, when he did the act, the fact that his own life or personal safety was in danger was not known to him. Following the growth of interest in justification and excuse, Professor Williams has modified his views.[36] The use of force is, he now thinks, justified as force used in self-defence if facts warranting the use of such force exist, even though the defendant is unaware of them, but force used in self-defence is only excused if the defendant believes wrongly, though perhaps reasonably, that facts exit which, had they existed, would have warranted the use of that force.

This has what you might think to be the rather odd result that the person who acts with *mens rea* (because he is unaware of the circumstances of justification) is said to be justified; whereas the person who acts without *mens rea* (because he believes in circumstances which, if true, excuse the use of force) is merely excused. But this is logically defensible because the theory is that it is the external facts which provide justification, irrespective of the actor's state of mind. What is truly odd is that the person said to be justified in killing or wounding, as the case may be, might now be convicted

[36] 2 *Legal Studies* 233 at p. 250.

of attempted murder or an attempt unlawfully to wound, under the Criminal Attempts Act 1981, as authoritatively interpreted by the House of Lords in *Shivpuri*,[37] whereas the person who is merely excused would not be guilty of anything. The principle of *Shivpuri* is that, for the purposes of the law of attempts, a person is to be treated as if the facts were as he believed them to be. If we treat the person who is unaware of the circumstances of justification as if those facts did not exist, he would, of course, be guilty of the offence in question. So he is guilty of an attempt. Professor Williams, however, sees[38] virtue in the fact that the "justified" defendant might now be convicted of an attempt: " . . . the point is that since a charge of attempt has become legally possible [sc., as a result of the Criminal Attempts Act 1981, as interpreted in *Shivpuri*] any argument of policy for convicting on the basis of a consummated crime has disappeared." It was Professor Williams's brilliantly persuasive writing[39] which induced the House of Lords to decide as they did in *Shivpuri*, overruling their own recent decision in *Anderton* v. *Ryan*,[40] and any opinion of his is entitled to the very greatest respect. But I venture to submit that, on this issue, a better view is that any argument of policy for *not* convicting of the consummated crime has disappeared. Can we sensibly say that, at one and the same time, a person is (i) justified in firing a gun at another with intent to kill him and (ii) guilty of attempted murder? Visualise the astonishment of the jury who, having heard how a latter-day Dadson deliberately fired at and wounded his victim, X, are directed that, on those facts, they should find him not guilty of unlawfully shooting at X with intent to cause him grievous bodily harm, but guilty of attempting unlawfully to shoot at X with intent to cause him

---

[37] [1987] A.C. 1.
[38] 2 *Legal Studies* 233 at p. 252.
[39] "The Lords and Impossible Attempts or Quis custodiet ipsos custodes?," [1986] *Cambridge Law Journal* 33.
[40] [1985] A.C. 560.

grievous bodily harm. "Policy" should surely determine whether this person is guilty of a crime, or of no crime. If, as a matter of policy, we think he was truly "justified" in doing what he did, it should be no crime. But if policy requires him to be convicted, it should surely be of the consummated crime. My own opinion is that policy requires his conviction.

2. Defences Express and Implied

Defences to Statutory Offences

Statutes creating criminal offences commonly include in the definition of the offence the word, "unlawfully." The function of this word is sometimes said to be to ensure that the general defences provided by the criminal law will apply to the offence. The statute does not say anything about, for example, duress or self-defence but, if a particular defendant was acting under duress or by way of self-defence, he was not acting unlawfully and so did not commit the offence. Sometimes the definition of the offence includes the phrase, "without lawful authority or excuse." This seems to be much the same in effect. A person who has "lawful authority or excuse" for what he does is not acting "unlawfully."

There is no consistency about the use of terminology of this kind[1] and there are many statutory offences where no such word or phrase is used. The section simply prohibits certain conduct without any express qualification. But it seems

[1] See the valuable discussion by Richard Card in [1969] Crim.L.R., 359 and 415.

to make no difference. The general defences apply in just the same way. In a case in 1986 a man called Renouf drove his car so as to ram another car, a Volvo, and force it off the road. He was charged with causing criminal damage to the Volvo and with reckless driving. The jury acquitted him of criminal damage but convicted him of reckless driving.[2] On those bare facts, the jury were no doubt entirely justified in convicting him of the driving offence. He drove so as to create an obvious and serious risk of causing physical harm to the occupants of the Volvo and of damage to it. It appeared in evidence at the trial, however, that, shortly before the incident which led to the charges, the Volvo had drawn up in the forecourt of Mr. Renouf's garage and the occupants had thrown various articles at him, damaging his car and causing him actual bodily harm. They then drove off with Mr. Renouf in hot pursuit. He rammed the Volvo and forced it off the road in order to arrest the occupants. As we have seen, section 3 of the Criminal Law Act 1967 entitles any person to use reasonable force to arrest another who has committed an arrestable offence—and criminal damage and assault occasioning actual bodily harm are arrestable offences.

Mr. Renouf appealed against his conviction and relied on section 3. The Criminal Damage Act uses the words, "without lawful excuse," and the Court of Appeal thought that the reason why the jury acquitted of criminal damage must have been that they thought that section 3 provided Renouf with a lawful excuse. But section 2 of the Road Traffic Act 1972, which creates the offence of reckless driving, uses no such words and the prosecution argued that their absence shut out any possibility of a defence under section 3 of the 1967 Act. The Court was not impressed with that argument. Lawton L.J. pointed out that section 20 of the Offences against the Person Act 1861 (maliciously wounding or inflicting grievous bodily harm) does not use that phrase either but section 3 has

[2] *R.* v. *Renouf* [1986] 1 W.L.R. 522.

been held to provide a defence to charges under that section. Section 20 does, however, use the word, "unlawfully." Section 2 of the Road Traffic Act does not even use that word. Nevertheless, the Court held that the defence provided by section 3 could apply to reckless driving. Forcing the Volvo off the road could be the "use of force" within the meaning of the 1967 Act and the judge ought to have left it to the jury to decide whether the force which Mr. Renouf used was reasonable in the circumstances.

The only real function of the word or phrase, then, appears to be to act as a reminder to the court that the criminal prohibition is not so absolute as it appears to be and is always subject to the general defences, unless they are expressly or impliedly excluded. But it is only a reminder and has no substantive effect. Parliament sometimes give the reminder and sometimes it does not. There is no consistent usage.

"Lawful" and "Reasonable" Excuse

There is, however, another phrase which is in common use and which does apparently extend the range of possible defences. This phrase is "without *reasonable* excuse. When "reasonable" is used instead of "lawful" this suggests that the excuse does not have to be one which is recognised by the general law. It is enough that it is reasonable. "Lawful" sends the reader to look for some law which will excuse. "Reasonable" does not. It would be a mistake, however, to suppose that the effect is that anything that you or I, the Common People, might think to be a reasonable excuse, is one. The judges exercise a strict degree of control over the application of these words by juries and magistrates. The judge may direct the jury as to what is, and, more importantly, what is not, capable of being a reasonable excuse; and the Divisional Court will overturn the decision of a magistrates' court which gives the phrase a too strict or a too generous interpretation.

Under the Prevention of Crime Act 1953 a person commits an offence if, "without lawful authority or reasonable excuse, the proof whereof shall lie on him," he has with him in any public place any offensive weapon." And an offensive weapon is "any article made or adapted for causing injury to the person, or intended by the person having it with him for such use by him." In *Evans* v. *Hughes*[3] the defendant who was carrying a "quite light" metal bar about six inches long was charged with an offence under this Act. The justices found that he had reasonable cause to fear, and did fear, that he would be violently attacked and that he was carrying it with him for self-defence only and not for an aggressive purpose. The justices thought, wrongly, that the bar was not an offensive weapon, but they went on to say that, even if it was an offensive weapon, the defendant had a reasonable excuse for having it with him. It was only with considerable hesitation that the court dismissed the prosecution's appeal. They stated the principle to be as follows:

" . . . in order that it may be a reasonable excuse to say, 'I carried this for my own defence,' the threat for which this defence is required must be an imminent particular threat affecting the particular circumstances in which the weapon was carried."

No doubt there are sound reasons of policy for restricting the meaning of "reasonable excuse" in this way. The effectiveness of the Act in keeping offensive weapons off the streets might be seriously impaired if everyone who reasonably feared that he might be attacked at some time was allowed to carry an offensive weapon. However good the motives of the

---

[3] [1972] 1 W.L.R. 1452.

carriers, the more weapons that are carried on the streets, the greater is the chance that they will be used.

Another example is to be found in the legislation relating to drinking and driving. A person who, without reasonable cause, fails to provide a specimen when required to do so in accordance with the provisions of the Road Traffic Act commits an offence. Here again, "reasonable excuse" has been strictly interpreted by the courts. It has been said by the Court of Appeal that no excuse can be judged to be reasonable unless the person from whom the specimen is required is physically or mentally unable to provide it, or the provision of the specimen would entail a substantial risk to his health.[4] It is possible that the law is not quite so strict as that but it is clear that it is by no means left open to a jury or magistrates to make their own judgment in all cases whether an alleged excuse is reasonable or not. As always, the courts' opinion on policy underlies their approach. We all need protection against the drinking driver and it is feared that a liberal interpretation of "reasonable excuse" would let too many offenders slip through the net. The judges are the guardians of public policy and it is their duty to take a longer and broader view than the jury dealing with a particular case.

It appears then that the effect of the phrase, "without reasonable excuse," in a statute is to give the court an authority, which it might otherwise lack, to add to the generally recognised defences to crime. The majority of statutory definitions of offences do not, however, include that phrase. The implication is that existence of what you or I, the Common People, a jury or magistrates, or even the judges themselves, might think to be reasonable excuse is not an excuse in law, unless it comes within one of the recognised defences. Some

---

[4] *John (Graham)* [1974] 2 All E.R. 561. (Religious beliefs, however sincerely held, could not, in law, amount to an excuse for failing to supply a specimen.) And see *Cotgrove* v. *Cooney* [1987] Crim.L.R. 272 and commentary.

may think that a defect in our law. Conviction of a criminal offence is, or certainly ought to be, a very serious matter; and it might be thought that there is something wrong if a person is liable to conviction when all reasonable people would say that he had a reasonable excuse for doing what he did. A partial answer to this criticism is that it is the almost invariable practice of Parliament to fix a maximum but no minimum sentence for each offence so, with rare exceptions like treason and murder, the court can give the offender an absolute discharge if it considers him blameless. But this is only a partial answer and the absolutely discharged defendant may have a legitimate grievance. Such defendants sometimes think it worth while to appeal against their convictions. There are, however, ways in which the courts may sometimes ensure the acquittal of the person who has apparently contravened the letter of the law, but has behaved reasonably in all the circumstances. The fault element of the offence is sometimes a useful vehicle for this approach.

Reasonable Excuse and Dishonesty

It has long been stated in the law books that necessity cannot be a defence to a charge of theft—that it is no answer for a man charged with stealing a loaf of bread to say that he took it because he and his family were starving. The authoritative seventeenth century writer, Hale,[5] justified this rule on the ground that the law of England made provision for the poor so that it never could be necessary to steal. But even if we accept that our social arrangements were and are so satisfactory, it does not follow that occasions may not arise when it is in fact necessary to appropriate another's property in order to preserve life or health. An example that is discussed in the

[5] 1 Hale P.C. 54.

literature (and in the Canadian case of *Perka*[6]) is that of a lost mountaineer who comes across an unoccupied hut, breaks in and, in order to keep himself alive, eats the food he finds there. In the unlikely event of such a person being charged with theft today, he would probably be well advised to eschew the defence of necessity and rely instead on the word, "dishonestly," in section 1 of the Theft Act 1968. Dishonesty is an essential element of theft. The Act does not provide a definition of dishonesty but it gives some instances of what is not to be regarded as dishonesty. Section 2(1)(b) tells us that a person's appropriation of property belonging to another is not to be regarded as dishonest—

> "if he appropriates the property in the belief that he would have the other's consent if the other knew of the appropriation and the circumstances of it."

The starving mountaineer probably would believe that the owner of the food would have given his consent had he known of the taker's predicament. If the mountaineer has done damage by breaking a window or forcing a lock and is charged with an offence of criminal damage, he could rely on a similar provision in the Criminal Damage Act 1971, section 5(2)(*a*), that a person is to be treated as having a lawful excuse for damaging property if he believes that the person entitled to consent to damage to the property would have consented had he known of the circumstances.

Suppose, however, that the owner of the hut has made it very clear that he does not consent to anyone entering in any circumstances. It is his own refuge in emergencies and will be of little use to him if his supplies are all gone. So the place is plastered with notices that trespassers will be prosecuted, whatever the circumstances of their entry. If the starving mountaineer sees the notices and knows that the owner does

[6] Above, p. 14.

not consent, can he still claim that he was not acting "dishonestly" within the meaning of the Theft Act? The Act does not tell us the answer and the courts have held that the question whether a person's conduct was dishonest is generally a question of fact for a jury. They must ask themselves, was the mountaineer's conduct dishonest according to the ordinary standards of reasonable and honest people? And, if it was, did the mountaineer know this? Only if the jury answer both questions in the affirmative is the defendant to be found guilty of dishonesty.[7]

The jury is subject to some measure of control by the judge. He must direct them so that they do not reach a result which is contrary to law; and he might reason that, since for so long it has been the law that necessity cannot justify or excuse theft, it follows that necessity cannot, in law, negative dishonesty. Or he might think it implicit in the Act that a taker who knows that the owner would not consent to the taking is to be regarded as dishonest. These are not negligible arguments, but I suspect they would not prevail. The judge would probably leave the question to the jury and it is surely unlikely that they would be satisfied that the starving mountaineer was dishonest. But this is not an entirely satisfactory solution to the problem for the definition of criminal damage does not include the word, "dishonestly." It includes the phrase, "without lawful excuse," and this phrase, like "dishonestly" in the Theft Act, is only partially defined. Section 5 of the Criminal Damage Act gives examples of lawful excuse but provides (section 5(5)), "This section shall not be construed as casting any doubt on any defence recognised by law as a defence to criminal charges." Thus, so far as criminal damage is concerned, we seem to come back in the end to the question whether necessity is recognised by law as a defence, a matter to which we shall return.

---

[7] *Ghosh* [1982] Q.B. 1053, C.A.

Reasonable Excuse and Recklessness

In many crimes the fault element required by the law is recklessness. The prosecution must prove that the defendant
behaved recklessly—that is, he took an unreasonable risk of
causing some result which the criminal law seeks to prevent.
There are some risks which it is reasonable to take and we
would not describe the taker of a reasonable risk as reckless.
A surgeon who performs a serious operation may be aware
that there is a grave risk that the operation will kill his
patient; but, if he knows that the patient will die soon unless
he has the operation and that there is a reasonable possibility
that his life may be substantially prolonged if the operation
succeeds, the risk, taken with the patient's consent, is justifiable. It is reasonable to take the risk. If the patient dies on
the operating table, we will not say that the surgeon has
killed him recklessly. So, in offences requiring recklessness,
there is a built-in defence of reasonableness. If, in all the circumstances of the case, the defendant was acting reasonably,
he was not reckless and is not guilty.

Whether it is reasonable to take a risk depends on whether
the social value of the activity outweighs the risk of causing
the harm in question—as the value of the operation may outweigh the risk of causing death in the case of the surgeon.
There can be no doubt that this is a principle of the law,
though it finds little application in the reported cases. The
reason is that most of the activities that result in criminal proceedings based on recklessness have no social value whatever
so there is nothing to weigh against and justify the risk.

The justification for taking a risk of causing harm to
another may be found in the public interest in sport and ath-
letic prowess. When boxers fight in accordance with the
Queensberry rules, there is, as everyone knows, some risk
that serious bodily harm or even death may be caused. If
death does result from a blow struck in such a fight the

surviving boxer is not guilty of murder or manslaughter or any offence. Reckless killing is manslaughter but, while the boxer has certainly taken some risk of causing, and has caused, the death of another, he has not done so recklessly because the prevailing opinion in our society considers it a reasonable risk to take.

Professor A. T. H. Smith is critical[8] of this analysis. He writes:

" . . . it places too great an emphasis on the fault element in criminal liability and insufficient on the element of justification. It may well be that the surgeon who takes a justified risk is not at fault, but it does not follow that he is acquitted for that reason. We absolve him from responsibility because the kind of conduct in which he engages is socially beneficial or at least (in the case of the boxer) not sufficiently harmful to warrant proscription. It is not, in short, unlawful, and he is justified in doing what he does however dubious his motives and intentions may be,"

This is a very persuasive view but it is not surprising that it is not the orthodox statement of the law. It is one thing to say that a surgeon may take a risk of killing his patient and that a boxer may take a risk of killing his opponent. It is quite another to say that either of them is justified in *intentionally* killing another person. A suggestion that this is the law might be expected to cause a public outcry. Suppose a boxer so hates his opponent that he hopes he will kill him but he fights fairly within the Queensberry rules and delivers a heavy blow, but a blow permitted by those rules, which kills, as he hoped it would. If he is charged with manslaughter and the indictment alleges that he killed his opponent recklessly, he appears, at first sight at least, to have a clear answer to the charge. Whatever his state of mind, he did nothing wrong.

---

[8] "On *Actus Reus* and *Mens Rea*," in *Reshaping the Criminal Law* (ed., Glazebrook, 1978) 95 at p. 101.

The risk of causing death which is involved in fighting in accordance with the rules is acceptable. If the objective element in recklessness cannot be established, the question of his state of mind need never arise. The prosecution falls at the first fence. Suppose, however, that he is charged with murder and the indictment alleges that he intentionally killed his opponent. He killed him all right; and, since he wanted to kill him, he intended to do so, whatever definition of intention is applied. That is murder, unless there are circumstances of justification or excuse. It would be very odd indeed if the same circumstances which afforded a defence to the less serious charge of manslaughter should not afford a defence to the graver charge of murder. A verdict of "Not guilty of murder but guilty of manslaughter" makes sense and is common enough; but a verdict of "Not guilty of manslaughter but guilty of murder" is absurd. If the blow is justified when the charge is manslaughter, why is it not justified when the charge is murder?

An exactly analogous problem may arise with the surgeon. He performs a highly dangerous but medically justifiable operation with the patient's informed consent and with all the great skill at his command—but secretly hoping that the operation will cause the patient's death so that he can marry the widow. If the operation does cause the patient's death, the surgeon has intentionally killed him.

Only in very exceptional circumstances, of course, would it be possible to prove the state of mind of either the boxer or the surgeon. If he kept his secret thoughts to himself, there would be no question of criminal liability. But perhaps he has been so rash as to record his wish to cause death in a diary or confided it to a friend. Professor Smith's opinion[9] is that—

" . . . it is most doubtful whether, as our law currently stands, the doctor or the boxer could plead that his

[9] *Ibid.*

conduct was justified. . . . Yet according to our current social and legal mores he has done nothing wrong. To convict the boxer [or, it may be added, the surgeon] in such circumstances would be to convict him for his evil thoughts."

So Professor Smith thinks that the surgeon and the boxer ought, in principle, to have a defence, ("according to our social *and legal* mores," they have done nothing wrong) but for some, not entirely clear, reason, they would be convicted. If, however, we accept that their conduct is justified, irrespective of their state of mind, it is impossible theoretically to justify the conviction of either of them. But there is, something highly suspect about a rule which, if it were spelled out in express terms, would almost certainly be rejected by society. A codifier of the criminal law would surely consider it futile to formulate such a rule—worse than futile, because not only would it be thrown out by Parliament, but it would tend to bring the Code into disrepute.

The only way out of this difficulty is to conclude that the circumstances of justification are not purely objective but do include the state of mind of the actor: that the surgeon is justified in inserting his scalpel into the body of his patient only if his *purpose* is to promote the life and health of the patient; and that the blow struck by the boxer is not justified if it is his purpose to cause a degree of harm greater than that which the law regards as tolerable. An intention to cause actual bodily harm—a black eye or a bloody nose—is acceptable because such minor harms are currently regarded as acceptable incidents of boxing. If causing unconsciousness is serious bodily harm then we are compelled to the conclusion that even an intention cause "grievous bodily harm," as it is still technically known in law, is acceptable, because there is nothing unlawful in the boxer knocking his opponent out—that is the object of the exercise—so there cannot be anything unlawful in his intending to do so. But an intention to kill is another matter.

What would be nonsensical would be to exempt the defendant from liability for manslaughter because he was not reckless and to hold him liable for murder because he intended to kill. The greater must include the less. The theory tentatively advanced above would leave the defendant who intended to kill liable to conviction of whichever offence was charged.

I can imagine that this argument might be countered by some such example as the following. A waiter in a restaurant, having been roundly abused by a customer for the delay in serving his fish, eventually delivers it with the heartfelt words, "I hope it chokes you." Unknown to the waiter, the fish contains a vicious bone on which the diner chokes and dies. Of course it would be absurd to convict the waiter of murder. However violent his thoughts as he delivered the lethal dish, he was only doing his lawful job as a waiter. Were not the surgeon and the boxer the same? I suggest not. Sticking a scalpel into someone or punching him on the jaw is not an ordinary, everyday, generally harmless action like serving food. It is wounding or assault—unless there are circumstances to justify it; and there is no reason why the law should not require, among the circumstances of justification, the appropriate intention, or at least the absence of an inappropriate intention, on the part of the actor.

Judicial Caution in Applying "Reasonable, therefore not Reckless"

I have suggested that, in principle, recklessness involves a "built-in" defence of reasonableness but I have to admit that there is not much authority for this proposition in the reported cases. The courts have been slow, or reluctant, to recognise and act on it. In *Renouf*,[10] the case of the man who

---

[10] Above, p. 46.

rammed the Volvo in order to arrest the occupants, the Court
of Appeal quashed the conviction because they recognised
that a properly directed jury might have found that the
defendant had a defence to the charge of reckless driving;
but it seems that the defence would have been, not that he
was not reckless, but that, even if he was reckless, he could
rely on section 3 of the Criminal Law Act 1967 to justify or
excuse his recklessness. As we have seen,[11] section 3 justifies
the use of reasonable force to make a lawful arrest and Mr.
Renouf was, or may have been, (it was for the jury to decide
and they had not been given the opportunity to do so) using
such force to make a lawful arrest. It is curious that the
defence was available only because the alleged reckless driving consisted in the use of force. One might have thought
that using force against another vehicle was a most aggravated form of reckless driving and, therefore, the last to be
excused. But section 3 authorises the use of reasonable force.
It does not, in terms, authorise the arrester to do anything
else which is prima facie unlawful. In the opinion of the
Court, it did not justify or excuse any "reckless" acts which
the defendant might have done before using force to stop the
Volvo. If, while driving in hot pursuit, Renouf had rounded a
bend at excessive speed, so as to create an obvious and
serious danger to other road users, had any been there (even
if, in fact, there were none) the Court would not, it seems,
have listened to an argument that it was reasonable in the circumstances to take this risk. Still less could there have been a
defence to a charge of exceeding the speed limit or going
through a red light. Such offences do not require recklessness
so an argument that it was reasonable to take any risks
involved could not have got off the ground.

There is, however, one decision by a Divisional Court
which is put expressly on the ground that conduct could not
be reckless because it was reasonable. This is the case of

[11] Above, p. 9.

Sears v. *Broome*[12] in 1986. The defendant was charged with
(i) causing criminal damage by breaking the window, valued
at £250, of an antique shop belonging to a Mr. Wood; and (ii)
assault occasioning actual bodily harm to a Mr. Thomas. His
defence was that Thomas had attacked him, that he was acting in self-defence and that, in doing so, he had knocked
Thomas through the window. The magistrates found him not
guilty of the assault because they were not satisfied that the
prosecution had proved (the onus of proof being on them)
that he was not acting reasonably in self-defence; but they
convicted him of criminal damage, holding that he had acted
recklessly in causing damage to the window. A single act by
the defendant caused both bodily harm to Thomas and
damage to Wood's window; and the magistrates were saying
that the act was lawful with respect to the first result but not
with respect to the second. The Divisional Court quashed the
conviction for criminal damage. They thought that it was
inconsistent to say that the defendant was acting reasonably
in self-defence yet acting recklessly—*i.e.* unreasonably,—in
damaging the window. Conduct cannot be both reasonable
and unreasonable at the same time.

While I welcome the recognition in that case of the
requirement that reckless conduct be unreasonable and do
not quarrel with the actual decision, I think some qualifications need to be made. First, the two charges involved different defences. The defence to the charge of assault was
plainly self-defence; but this can scarcely have been the
defence to the charge of breaking the window. The window
belonged, not to the alleged aggressor, Thomas, but to the
innocent Mr. Wood. It was merely his misfortune that the
fight happened to take place outside his shop. The defence to
the charge of breaking the window was rather in the nature
of a defence of necessity—it was necessary for the defendant
to damage the property of an innocent third party in order to

[12] [1986] Crim.L.R. 461.

protect himself from bodily injury. The courts do not expressly recognise any general defence of necessity, but, as I shall try to show later, such a defence is sometimes found concealed in other concepts. Here it was concealed in the notion of recklessness. If the defendant in *Sears* v. *Broome* had realised that it was certain that he would break the window and had been charged with intentionally doing so, the recklessness escape route would not have been open and the court would have been forced expressly to consider necessity as a defence.

Secondly, I do not think it can be maintained as a general proposition that conduct which is reasonable with respect to a person responsible for aggression is also necessarily reasonable with respect to innocent third parties. Suppose that, while I am out grouse shooting, I am attacked by your large and ferocious dog. It may well be that, fearing injury to my person and having a shot-gun under my arm, I would be justified in shooting at the animal and killing or wounding it. If you prosecuted me for causing criminal damage to your property, a valuable dog, I would have a defence to the charge. I was acting in reasonable self-defence.

Suppose, however, that, as I raised the gun to point it at the charging animal, I realised that my friend, George, was directly in the line of sight and would almost inevitably be peppered with shot if I pulled the trigger. If I do pull it, do I have a defence to a charge of unlawfully wounding George? Clearly, I cannot rely on self-defence against my unlucky friend. If I have no defence to the charge of unlawful wounding, does it follow that the act of pulling the trigger was unlawful and that I have no defence to the charge of criminal damage to the dog? I suggest that this does not follow and that a single act may be a reasonable act to do with respect to one of its foreseen consequences but not with respect to others. In circumstances of this kind, it is not possible to consult one's solicitor but if, by some magic, it were possible and if, as the dog charged, I were to ask him, "Is it lawful to pull the trigger," he would have to answer, "Yes and no," which I would not find awfully helpful. It would, I suggest, be perfectly proper for a judge to leave it to a jury to convict me of unlawful wounding if they thought it unreasonable to shoot, or to take the risk of shooting, George, while at the same time acquitting me of criminal damage to the dog, if they thought it was reasonable in the circumstances to shoot it. Since there is, or ought to be, a higher interest in protecting the person than in protecting property, it may be that any force which is reasonable, though it injures the person, is prima facie also reasonable with respect to property—which was the issue in *Sears* v. *Broome*—but the converse does not follow.

Concealed Defences

Perhaps because of a reluctance to recognise general defences, especially the defence of necessity, our courts have sometimes relied on a manipulation of one or other of the basic concepts of the criminal law to achieve the same result. The most striking example is the case of *Steane*[13] in 1947. Steane, a British subject, had the misfortune to fall into the hands of the Nazis during the second world war. He had been held in a concentration camp where he was subjected to brutal treatment. After being released from the camp, he was instructed to make broadcasts favourable to the German cause and told that, if he did not do so, he and his wife and family would go back to the concentration camp. So he read the scripts provided. After the war he was charged, not with treason, but with a lesser offence under the Defence Regulations, "doing an act likely to assist the enemy with intent to assist the enemy." It was quite clear that reading the script was an act "likely to assist the enemy" within the meaning of

[13] [1947] K.B. 997.

this regulation because "assist the enemy" plainly means assist in the enemy's plans, whether they be good plans or bad ones. But Steane argued that he had no intent to assist the enemy. He was a loyal citizen who had no wish to assist Nazi Germany. He read the script solely in order to save himself and his family from the horrors of the concentration camp. This argument was accepted by the Court of Criminal Appeal which quashed his conviction. Lord Goddard C.J. said that the jury should have been told that they would be entitled to presume the required intent if they thought that the act was done as the result of the free, uncontrolled action of the accused; but they would not be entitled to presume it if the circumstances showed that the act was done in subjection to the power of the enemy or was as equally consistent with an innocent intent—an intention to save his wife and children from the concentration camp—as with a criminal intent. Lord Goddard expressly put aside any possible defence of duress. It was not necessary to consider that defence unless and until the prosecution had proved intent. But Steane undoubtedly intended to read the script, however reluctantly he did so; and reading the script *was* assisting the enemy. If the regulation had provided that it should be an offence to broadcast enemy scripts, it seems very improbable that the defence of lack of intention could have succeeded, because it is so very obvious that Steane, excusably or not, did intend to read the scripts.

Suppose, to borrow an example from Professor Glanville Williams,[14] that Steane had been a chain smoker and that his supply of cigarettes had been cut off. He had been told that it would be restored if he gave the broadcast. Being desperate for a smoke, he did so. Imagine the reaction of that stern judge, Lord Goddard, to a defence that the defendant's only intent was to get back his cigarette supply, not to assist the enemy. I have no doubt that the defence would have been

[14] (1965) *The Mental Element in Crime* p. 23.

summarily and contemptuously dismissed. There is, of course, a great moral difference betwen the real case and the hypothetical one; but so far as the concept of intention is concerned, there is no difference. In both cases, the act of reading the script has two foreseen and inseparable consequences: (i) it assists the enemy; and (ii) it either provides salvation from the concentration camp or it restores the cigarette supply. The defendant in neither case wants to bring about the first consequence but he wants the second and, as he knows, inseparable consequence so badly that he decides to bring about both. In relying on the concept of intention to excuse Steane, the Court made it carry a burden which it cannot properly bear. The Court ought to have fallen back on the defence of duress. This would almost certainly have afforded a defence to Steane but not to the hypothetical chain smoker, because the law limits strictly the type of threat which it regards as constituting duress.

It is perhaps worth digressing to consider the decision in *Steane* in the light of the principle that superior orders, even the orders of a tyrannical government with overwhelming power, are not a defence to a criminal charge. Article 8 of the Nuremberg statute (Charter of the International Military Tribunal (1945) (annex to TS 27 (1946); Cmd. 6903) states that:

"The fact that Defendant acted pursuant to order of his government or of a superior shall not free him from responsibility, but may be considered in mitigation of punishment if the Tribunal determines that justice so requires."

Lord Hailsham said[15] in the recent case of *Howe and Bannister* that this statement was "universally accepted, save for its reference to mitigation, as an accurate statement of the common law both in England and the United States of

[15] [1987] A.C. at p. 427.

America." His Lordship also pointed out that "superior orders" is not identical with duress but, in the circumstances of the Nazi regime, "the difference must often have been negligible." If, however, the defendant who acted under superior orders backed by the threat of death or serious bodily harm is able to say that he intended only to save his skin and therefore did not intend the criminal result with which he is charged, the way is open for the evasion of the rule. But in *Howe and Bannister* their Lordships did not accept that duress negatives the intention to commit the forbidden act. On the contrary, Lord Hailsham cited with approval the statement of Lord Kilbrandon in the earlier case of *Lynch*[16]:

> " . . . the decision of the threatened man whose constancy is overborne so that he yields to the threat, *is a calculated decision to do what* he knows to be wrong . . . "

Steane's decision to read the scripts was no doubt a calculated decision to do just that; and therefore a calculated decision to do an act of assistance to the enemy. He may well have considered that he was not doing "wrong" in any moral sense. He may have thought that the prospects of the broadcasts doing any actual harm to his country were negligible— the more notorious broadcasts of William Joyce, "Lord Haw-Haw," were widely regarded as a joke (but he was hanged for them)—and that very real harm was certain to result to himself and his family if he did not comply. But that cannot absolve him from an "intent to assist the enemy."

Concealed Necessity—Gillick's Case

Because duress is an established defence, readily applicable in circumstances such as those of *Steane*, there was absolutely no need to strain the concept of intention in order to achieve

---

[16] [1975] A.C. at p. 428. (Lord Hailsham's italics.)

a just result. But the courts have yet to recognise a general defence of necessity and here we sometimes find the judges, with perhaps more reason, restricting the meaning of intention in a particular case in such a way as to compensate for the lack of such a defence. In Mrs. Gillick's case[17] in 1985, a civil action, the question was "whether a doctor may ever, in any circumstances, lawfully give contraceptive advice or treatment to a girl under the age of sixteen without her parents' consent." The House of Lords decided that a doctor may, in certain carefully prescribed conditions, lawfully give such advice or treatment. The relevance to the criminal law of this decision is that it is an offence for a man to have sexual intercourse with a girl under the age of 16. The girl does not commit an offence, even though she is a willing party to the intercourse, even, indeed, if she incites and encourages it. The general principle is that anyone who knowingly assists or encourages the commission of a criminal offence is guilty as an "aider and abettor" of that offence, when it is committed, and is liable to conviction as if he were the principal offender. The girl is exempt from this rule because the offence exists for her protection—she is regarded as a victim, not a party—but the general law of secondary participation in crime applies to anyone else who assists or encourages the commission of the offence by the man.

Now it is apparent that the provision of contraceptive advice and assistance to the girl may facilitate the commission of the offence by the man. Lord Brandon, dissenting in the result, went so far as to say that such advice or treatment necessarily promotes or encourages the sexual intercourse because it largely removes the inhibition of the risk of an unwanted pregnancy. If giving advice or treatment amounted to aiding and abetting an offence it was itself a crime and could not be lawful, whether the parents consented

---

[17] *Gillick* v. *West Norfolk and Wisbech Area Health Authority* [1986] A.C. 112, H.L.

or not. It is implicit in the decision of the majority that the doctor's advice and treatment, when the stated conditions are satisfied, does not amount to an offence. But why? It is no answer to a charge of aiding and abetting that the offence was going to be committed anyway. The defendant is still liable if he encouraged or facilitated the commission of an offence which would have occurred even if he had not intervened. Nor is it an answer that the offender, the man, might never know of the doctor's act—one who in fact facilitates the commission of an offence may be guilty of aiding and abetting its commission, although the offender is never aware that he was assisted. If the doctor's action encouraged the girl more readily to take part in the intercourse, he aided and abetted the commission of the offence by the man, although the man knew nothing of it.

The decision of the majority assumes that the hypothetical doctor is innocent, apparently on the ground that he would lack the necessary intent. The judge of first instance, Woolf J., whose opinions on this aspect of the case were adopted by two of their Lordships, recognised that a doctor who provided contraceptive advice to the girl or the man "with the intention of encouraging them to have sexual intercourse" would be guilty of an offence. Clearly, he thought that the hypothetical doctor, giving advice and treatment in the interests of his patient, the girl, would have no such intention. He also recognised that where a person gives encouragement to the commission of an offence, "an unimpeachable motive is no answer." Now when a person knows that a consequence is virtually certain to follow from his conduct there is a sufficient case to leave to a jury that he intended that consequence. It is for the jury to say, in the end, whether that state of mind should be characterised as "intention"; but, so far as the law is concerned, no further evidence is required. A doctor who satisfies the conditions of legality laid down by the House may be well aware that the provision of contraception will certainly encourage both the girl and the man to have intercourse and that what is likely to happen anyway will become more likely to do so. Their Lordships certainly make no condition that the doctor should not be so aware. His motive is, no doubt, "unimpeachable"—he is acting in what he thinks to be, and probably what are, the best interests of the girl—but such excellent motives, as Woolf J. recognised, are no answer to the charge.

The real basis of the decision, in my opinion, is that, in the limited circumstances specified by the House, the aiding and abetting of the offence is justified as being a lesser evil than the alternative—that the girl will or may have sexual intercourse without contraception and with the risk of a pregnancy. I have described this as a "concealed defence of necessity." Not everyone agrees with this interpretation. It has been suggested that the explanation is that aiding and abetting requires a *purpose* of aiding and abetting the commission of the offence, which the bona-fide doctor clearly does not have; but there is authority[18] against such a narrow interpretation of aiding and abetting. A seller of contraceptives to 15 year old schoolgirls whose defence to a charge of aiding and abetting intercourse by a man with one of the girls was that his only purpose was to make a profit and that he was quite indifferent as to what the girls did with his goods would, I am sure, receive short shrift—and rightly so. But the doctor may be no less aware than the contraceptive vendor of the likely effects of his action. Mr. John Spencer[19] accepts the concealed necessity theory, remarking—

> "It is difficult to dissent from this—except to say that as both Lord Bridge and Lord Scarman reinforced their views with arguments on social policy, the defence of necessity was hardly very much concealed."

[18] *National Coal Board* v. *Gamble* [1959] 1 Q.B. 11 at p. 23, *per* Devlin J.; *Lynch* v. *D.P.P. for Northern Ireland* [1975] A.C. 653 at p. 678.
[19] "Trying to Help Another Person Commit a Crime," in *Criminal Law: Essays in Honour of J. C. Smith* (ed., P. F. Smith, 1987) 148 at p. 164.

And he quotes Lord Scarman:

"If the prescription is the bona fide exercise of his clinical judgment as to what is best for his patient's health, he has nothing to fear from the criminal law or from any public policy based on the criminality of a man having sexual intercourse with [a girl under the age of 16]."

Other Cases of "Concealed Necessity"

Unwanted pregnancies in young girls are a great evil; but an even greater evil is the disease of AIDS. It has been suggested[20] that, in order to prevent the spread of AIDS in men's prisons, the prisoners should be issued with contraceptives. But it is still an offence for two men, even if both are aged 21 or above, to commit buggery or gross indecency, otherwise than "in private" and it is doubtful whether an act in a prison cell could be regarded as done in private for this purpose. If, as is said to be common, there are three prisoners in the cell, the act is certainly not "in private." It seems indisputable that the supply of contraceptives would be an encouragement to the prisoners to commit the offence. If so, the supplier would, prima facie, be equally guilty of it because he could hardly fail to be aware of the effect of the supply. Could he plead that he intended only to prevent the spread of AIDS and did not intend to aid and abet the commission of homosexual offences? The case is very close in this respect to that of *Gillick* but it poses the issue more starkly. The supply would be to the prospective criminal himself and its only purpose would be to enable the prisoner to perpetrate the offence more safely. The supplier of a bullet-proof waistcoat to a man whom he knows to be a professional armed robber is, I suggest, plainly guilty of aiding any armed robbery which the robber perpetrates while wearing the waistcoat; and it would

---

[20] *HIV, AIDS and Prisons* (Prison Reform Trust), (1988) pp. 19–20.

be no answer for the supplier to assert, however truthfully, that his only purpose was to make a profit out of the sale and that he did not care what the buyer did with the waistcoat. It would be enough to condemn him that he knew that he was facilitating armed robbery. It is hard to see that the supply of the contraceptives to the prisoners is different in any material respect, so far as the ordinary law of participation in crime is concerned. If such a step is to be justified or excused, without distortion of the general concepts of the criminal law, it must be by virtue of a defence in the nature of necessity.

A similar problem is raised by the suggestion[21] that users of prohibited drugs should be issued with free syringes with the same object of reducing the spread of AIDS. A drug pusher who supplied the free syringes with the object of encouraging the use of the drugs he supplied would clearly be guilty of aiding and abetting offences by the drug addicts. The provision of the syringes would encourage the illegal acquisition and use of controlled drugs. No one would have any sympathy for the drug pusher if he were convicted. The same provision by the local health authority might be expected to have exactly the same effect. Of course, the authority's motives would be of the best, but, as we have seen, under the ordinary law, an unimpeachable motive is no answer. Yet the underlying basis of *Gillick's case*, if I have discerned it correctly, might again come to the rescue. The great evil of drug abuse might be thought to be outweighed by the still greater evil of AIDS, so that some encouragement of the former is permissible in order to reduce the impact of the latter.

It is unlikely that a court would recognise necessity in express terms but it is quite likely, in my opinion, that a court would justify an acquittal of the health authority by resorting to a narrow concept of intention, as in *Gillick*: the authority intends only to inhibit the spread of AIDS and has no intention

---

[21] *The Times*, June 3, 1986.

to aid and abet an offence. According to the ordinary principles of law, there would, in my opinion, be evidence that the authority had both intentions. If there is justification or excuse for the conduct of the hypothetical authority, it is a concealed defence of necessity.

A Concealed Defence of Superior Orders?

We have seen that it is generally accepted that superior orders cannot be a defence to crime. It is no answer for an employee who has done a criminal act to say that he was only obeying the instructions of his employer. Yet in a case in 1987, *R.* v. *Salford Health Authority ex p. Janaway*,[22] the Court of Appeal (Civil Division) held that a secretary who typed a letter arranging an illegal abortion would not be guilty of aiding and abetting the abortion, because she would only be doing what she was told to do. The question of criminal liability was not directly in issue, but the decision on the point appears to be part of the *ratio decidendi* of the case. The question was whether the secretary who had refused to type the letter was in breach of her contract of employment. Her argument was that she was not, because of section 4(1) of the Abortion Act 1967, which provides that no person is under a duty to participate in any treatment authorised by the Act to which he has a conscientious objection. She said she had a conscientious objection to abortion and therefore she was under no duty to write the letter. The contemplated abortion was not illegal because it was authorised by the Act but it would have been illegal before 1967. It was held that the secretary could rely on the conscientious objection clause only if she was being asked to do something which it would have been unlawful for her to do before 1967. So it was

[22] [1988] 2 W.L.R. 442, C.A., affirmed on other grounds, [1988] 3 W.L.R. 1350, H.L.

necessary to determine whether a secretary, instructed by her
employer to type a letter arranging a criminal abortion, would
be guilty of aiding and abetting the crime if she wrote the
letter. The court held that she would not. Slade L.J. said[23]:

> "Whatever might be said of the doctor whose letter she
> was being asked to type, she herself in typing it would have
> been merely intending to carry out the obligations of her
> employment and not endeavouring to produce a result
> consisting of an abortion. Thus she would . . . not have
> had the necessary intent to render her a procurer."

So, once again, we find the court invoking the concept of
intention in order to admit what is, in substance, a defence to
crime, by the back door—in this case the defence of superior
orders. Of course it is true that the secretary would not have
been "endeavouring" to cause an abortion; but to rely on
that to exclude liability ignores the fact that an intention to
give assistance is sufficient for liability. Would the court have
taken the same view, I wonder, if the secretary had been
asked to type a letter arranging a murder—a "contract killing" of the boss's wife for example? I very much doubt it.
Her defence, "I was only intending to carry out the obligations of my employment," would have met with the sharp
response that her obligations, in law, could not include
arranging murders. But, for this purpose, there is no material
difference between arranging murder and arranging an
illegal abortion—which is an offence punishable with life
imprisonment. The secretary's answer, that she did not
intend to assist in the murder would, I believe, have been
scornfully dismissed. The letter she intentionally typed
would, as she could scarcely fail to know, facilitate the per-
petration of the murder; and that is evidence upon which it
would be for a jury to say whether her state of mind was to be
characterised as intention. The murder case and the illegal

[23] At p. 452.

abortion case cannot be distinguished on the basis of the intention of the writer of the letter. I doubt if they are properly distinguishable at all. Was not the Court allowing a "back door" defence of superior orders in this case where the role of the typist was relatively insignificant and the letter she was being asked to type was of the same general character as the letters she was properly employed to type? But a criminal court, trying a secretary who had written letters arranging an abortion which she knew to be unlawful under the terms of the Abortion Act 1967, might feel some reluctance in following the *Salford Health Authority case.*

3. Necessity and Duress

Necessity: Killing One that Others May Live

At the inquest[1] into the deaths caused in the Zeebrugge dis-
aster evidence was given by one of the passengers in the
Herald of Free Enterprise, a corporal in the army, that he and
a number of other people, apparently dozens of them, were
in the water and in danger of drowning. But they were near
the foot of a rope ladder up which they might climb to safety.
On the ladder, petrified with cold or fear, or both, was a
young man, unable to move up or down. No one could get
past him. The corporal shouted at him for 10 minutes with no
effect. Eventually he instructed someone else who was
nearer to the young man to push him off the ladder. The
young man then was pushed off and he fell into the water
and, so far as is known, was never seen again. The corporal
and others were then able to climb up the ladder to safety.

It does not appear from the the transcript of the coroner's
summing-up whether anyone warned the corporal, when he

[1] Transcript of Zeebrugge Inquest, Coroner's summing-up, p. 5 of after-
noon proceedings for October 2, 1987.

73

gave his evidence, that he was not bound to incriminate himself and that this evidence might amount to an admission of murder; and yet, as the law is currently stated, by the highest judicial authority, the killing of the young man—and it seems highly probable that he *was* killed by being knocked into the icy water—was neither justifiable nor excusable. Indeed, the coroner, in discussing this incident, said, "I think we need at least to glance in the direction of murder . . . "—but he gave no more than a glance, for he went on to say that we do not know whether the man on the ladder survived and that there was no evidence of his identity and, indeed, some uncertainty whether he was a young or a middle-aged man. Of course there may be murder of a person unknown and it is immaterial whether he was young or middle-aged, but there must be clear proof that someone was in fact killed. The coroner said, "There simply isn't any evidence" and he added:

" . . . but even if there were, I would suggest to you that killing in a reasonable act of what is known as self-preservation, but that also includes, in my judgment, the preservation of other lives, such killing is not necessarily murder at all."

He went on to direct the jury, in effect, that there was no evidence of unlawful killing and, of course, there has been no suggestion that the corporal or any of the others involved in that incident should be prosecuted for murder or manslaughter. It would, in my opinion, be quite outrageous if there were. But, if there was evidence that the man on the ladder was in fact drowned as a result of being knocked off it, there is no authority for the proposition that this was a lawful thing to do. On the contrary, such authority as exists is to the effect that the killing of one to save the lives of others cannot be justified or even excused.

In the famous case of *Dudley and Stephens*[2] in 1884, three

---

[2] [1884] 14 Q.B.D. 273.

men and a boy were shipwrecked and cast adrift in an open boat with very little food and water. After 18 days when, as a jury subsequently found, there was no appreciable chance of saving life, except by killing one for the others to eat, two of the men killed the boy, who was in a much weaker condition than they, and all three fed on his body and were rescued four days later. Dudley and Stephens were convicted of murder. It was, it appears, no defence that the only way in which the lives of three could be saved was by killing the fourth. It is interesting to note that, while Lord Coleridge C.J. spoke in terms of both justification and excuse, he appears to have held that there could be no defence to the charge unless the defendants were actually justified in doing what they did—a judicial attitude, which I criticised in my first lecture. Lord Coleridge said[3]:

> "Now it is admitted that the deliberate killing of this unoffending and unresisting boy was clearly murder unless the killing can be *justified* by some well recognised excuse admitted by the law. It is further admitted that there was in this case no such excuse, unless the killing was justified by what has been called 'necessity.' But the temptation to the act which existed here was not what the law has ever called necessity. Nor is this to be regretted."

It has been questioned whether *Dudley and Stephens* was a true case of necessity because Lord Coleridge observed that the shipwrecked mariners "might possibly have been picked up next day by a passing ship; they might possibly not have been picked up at all; and in either case it is obvious that the killing of this boy would have been an unnecessary and profitless act." But in considering whether there is a true necessity we must look at the situation as it must have appeared to the persons involved at the time; and the jury had found that there was no appreciable chance of saving life except by killing. So it is not surprising that in the case of *Howe and*

[3] At pp. 286–287.

Bannister in 1987 the House of Lords has held that the court in *Dudley and Stephens* decided that necessity was no defence to the two shipwrecked and starving sailors. In *Howe and Bannister* the House was concerned with a case, not of necessity, but of duress, but they held that the same principles applied to the two defences. " . . . if we were to allow this appeal," said Lord Hailsham,[4] "we should, I think, also have to say that *R.* v. *Dudley and Stephens* was bad law." He was not prepared to say that. He held that *Dudley and Stephens* was good law. Lord Mackay said[5]:

> "The justification for allowing a defence of duress to a charge of murder is that a defendant should be excused who killed as the only way of avoiding death himself or preventing the death of some close relation such as his own well-loved child. This was essentially the dilemma which Dudley and Stephens faced and in denying their defence the court refused to allow this consideration to be used in a defence to murder. If that refusal was right in the case of Dudley and Stephens it cannot be wrong in the present appeals."

So the House appears to have decided that it is no defence to murder that the life of the deceased was taken in order to preserve the lives of three others—or, one must suppose, of four, or five—or a hundred, others. But, if I am right in my assumption that no one would, or should, dream of prosecuting the corporal on the *Herald* (even if it could be proved that the man on the ladder died when he was knocked into the water) there is surely something wrong. Can it really be the law that all those people were under a duty to die, together with the man on the ladder, when they could escape by knocking him off? I suspect that most of us, the Common People, would think that, far from being blamed, the cor-

<hr />

[4] [1987] A.C. 417 at p. 429.
[5] At p. 453.

poral was to be praised for what he did. That is, if it is really necessary to seek a justification as distinct from an excuse to found a defence, here there was justification. The law has lost touch with reality if it condemns as murder conduct which right-thinking people regard as praiseworthy.

But perhaps *Dudley and Stephens*, even as confirmed by *Howe and Bannister*, is not an insuperable obstacle to a just result. It might be distinguished on two grounds. First, in *Dudley and Stephens* Lord Coleridge C.J. asked[6]:

> "Who is to be the judge of this sort of necessity? By what measure is the comparative value of lives to be measured? Is it to be strength, or intellect, or what? It is plain that the principle leaves to him who is to profit by it to determine the necessity which will justify him in deliberately taking another's life to save his own. In this case the weakest, the youngest, the most unresisting, was chosen. Was it more necessary to kill him than one of the grown men? the answer must be 'No. . . . ' "

Professor Glanville Williams[7] considers this problem of choosing the victim to be the "one satisfying reason" in the judgment in *Dudley and Stephens*; and in the *Herald* case the problem of choice did not, of course, arise. The unfortunate man on the ladder chose himself by his immobility there. There was no question of deciding between him and another. So at least one reason for the decision in *Dudley and Stephens*, and perhaps the only good reason, does not apply.

The second distinguishing factor is related. The man on the ladder was obstructing the passage of the people below. Though he was in no way at fault, he was preventing them from going where they had a right, and a most urgent need, to go. He was, unwittingly, imperilling their lives. I am not, of course, suggesting that there is a general right to kill a

---

[6] [1884] 14 Q.B.D. 273. At p. 287.
[7] *The Criminal Law, The General Part*, 744.

person in order to prevent him causing an obstruction. Only reasonable force may be used to remove an obstruction and that will usually be only slight force. But what is reasonable depends on the circumstances. Where the consequences of the continuance of the obstruction may be fatal, the force which may be used to remove it should be proportionately great. Whether it should extend as far as deadly force is the question to be decided. If the court should rule that it can never be lawful to kill an innocent person to save the lives of others, then the matter would never get before a jury; but if, as I believe he should, the judge left the matter to them, it would be a question of whether they were satisfied that the force used was unreasonable in the circumstances, because the onus of proof would be on the prosecution. There is some analogy with the case of the aggressive nine-year-old I discussed in an earlier lecture. As you will recall, he was committing no crime, but it was lawful to use reasonable force, which might be deadly force, to ward off the danger he created.

So, if such a case ever did come before a court, it would not be too difficult, I believe, for the judge to distinguish *Dudley and Stephens*; and my own opinion is that he would be entirely right to do so. What would we think of a law which said that all the trapped passengers, including the man on the ladder, were bound to die, rather than knock him to his death? But, if they are not so bound, we have breached the supposed rule that necessity can never be a defence to a murder charge.

A similar type of case which has been much discussed in the books is that of a roped mountaineer who falls over a cliff and is in danger of dragging his companion or companions after him. May his companion cut the rope, sending his friend to immediate death? It is not just a hypothetical problem according to a recent book, *Touching the Void*,[8] which

---

[8] Jonathan Cape (1988), reviewed, the *Sunday Express*, July 3, 1988.

describes how a mountaineer, Joe Simpson, while climbing in the Andes, slipped off a 19,000-foot cliff edge and was left dangling on a rope. For an hour, his only companion, Simon Yates, held him, becoming more and more exhausted and numb with cold. If he clung on much longer, he too would go over the edge. He cut the rope and Simpson hurtled into space. Yates writes, "I might as well have put a gun to his head and shot him." But in fact it was not so, because, almost miraculously, Simpson landed on a snowy ice bridge 100 feet below the cliff edge and survived. When they met again, Simpson said to Yates, "You did right." Did he do right in law? Well, at least I would suggest that he did not do wrong. As in the *Herald* case, there was no question of choosing one of two or more innocent persons to die to save the other or others. The accident had chosen the unlucky Simpson. And, again, Simpson was imperilling Yates's life. Simpson was committing no offence and so far as appears, was not at fault in any way; but he imperilled Yates's life in the same way as the man on the ladder imperilled the lives of the other passengers on the *Herald*. And so, I suggest that, if it was necessary to cut the rope in order to save his own life, Yates would not have been guilty of murder or any offence, had Simpson's apparently inevitable death occurred.

Mercy-Killing

Another type of killing where the question of necessity may arise is the so-called "mercy-killing." But the law is clear that it is no defence to a charge of murder that the defendant killed the deceased only to spare him suffering and because of his love and compassion for him. The parent who smothers his suffering child because he cannot bear to watch the pain any more is, prima facie, just as guilty in law of murder as the grasping killer who poisons his victim in order to inherit his property. In August this year a 54-year-old man was convicted of murder and sentenced to life imprisonment, as the law requires, after he had killed his wife who was confined to a wheelchair, suffering from a wasting disease, and who had repeatedly begged to be put out of her misery.[9] Sometimes the mercy-killer is found by the jury to be not guilty of murder but guilty of manslaughter on the ground of diminished responsibility—they accept medical evidence which says that he was suffering from an abnormality of mind which substantially diminished his mental responsibility in doing the act of killing—but this often seems to be in the nature of a merciful fiction. Even then, the mercy-killer is far from being justified or excused in law, because he is convicted of an offence punishable with a maximum sentence of life imprisonment, though he will probably in fact receive a very lenient sentence.

In 1976 the Criminal Law Revision Committee made a very tentative proposal in a working paper that consideration should be given to the creation of a new offence of mercy-killing. The proposed offence would have applied to a person who, from compassion, unlawfully killed another person who was, or was with reasonable cause believed to be, (1) subject to great bodily pain or suffering, or (2) permanently helpless from bodily or mental incapacity or (3) subject to rapid and incurable bodily or mental degeneration. Notice that it was not proposed to legalise mercy-killing but only to provide that it should not be murder or manslaughter but this lesser offence, punishable with two years' imprisonment. But this proposal received a hostile reception. It was clear that public opinion was not prepared to countenance what was seen as a threat to the sanctity of life. When the Committee published their final report[10] on Offences against the Person, the proposal was abandoned. So there is confirmation, if confirmation

---

[9] *The Times*, August 16, 1988.
[10] CLRC, Fourteenth Report, Cmnd. 7844 (1980), at p. 53.

be needed, that, by English law, mercy-killing is, and ought to be, murder, in the absence of proof of an abnormality of mind amounting to diminished responsibility.

Once again, however, I want to question whether this is, or should be, the law in all circumstances. The question is raised by a recent British Medical Association publication, *Nuclear Attack: Ethics and Casualty Selection* (1988). This is concerned with the horrific problems which would face doctors after a nuclear attack. The authors write[11]:

" . . . it is clear that following attack there will be large numbers of people suffering pain and distress for whom no definitive treatment will be available. Doctors may face pressure from suffering casualties or their loved ones, to ease the death of those for whom survival is impossible."

Having observed that supplies of analgesics and sedatives will not be sufficient to offer normal standards of palliative care to the dying and that doctors will have to determine the most humane way of allocating resources within the community of the suffering, the authors continue:

"In the United Kingdom it is widely accepted that the duty to preserve life does not extend to using every possible medical intervention in terminally ill patients where this will cause undue distress and discomfort. Equally, it does not require that distressing symptoms can never be relieved if treatment carries an incidental risk of shortening the terminally ill patient's life. However, deliberate acts, performed with the specific intent of terminating a person's life, are not only criminal but in our view inexcusable other than in wholly exceptional circumstances such as could not arise in the ordinary run of medical practice."

So the B.M.A. working party envisages that, "in wholly exceptional circumstances"—of which the most obvious

[11] At p. 65.

instance is the nuclear attack they are concerned with—it would be at least excusable deliberately to kill a terminally ill patient whose suffering could not be relieved. The working party was not, and did not purport to be, a committee expert in the law; but their opinion, as a group of eminent doctors, deserves the highest respect in a matter of this kind. If, in their view, the conduct is excusable, a law which declares it to be murder is, at least, highly suspect. They stress that only certain knowledge that the victim would experience terrible suffering could justify the mercy-killer—that mercy-killing "can be condoned only where the strongest humanitarian motives act in accord with a firm and indeed incontestable factual condition." In support of their opinion, they refer[12] to the Army Medical Services record of the Second World War Burma campaign which:

> " . . . give the overwhelming impression . . . that everything possible was done to evacuate all who could be evacuated and only when no other alternative could be contemplated were acts of mercy killing performed."

But it is clear that such acts were performed. A particular instance is described in the records of men who had suffered the most horrific injuries, for whom there was no hope and for whom no morphia was available. They were shot. Was that murder? I trust not; but if it is not, this can only be through the exercise of that residual power which Stephen J. thought the courts have and should continue to have, to allow new defences in unprecedented circumstances.

Relationship of Necessity to Duress

It is well established that duress is a general, though strictly limited defence to crime, but it is far from clear that necessity

[12] At p. 66.

is a general defence. This is one reason why the relationship between the two is of great importance. If the same principles apply to necessity as to duress, we are enabled to state the law of necessity more fully. Weight is given to the general condemnation of one of the least happy of the Law Commission's recommendations[13] for law reform—which was that there should be no general defence of necessity and that, for the avoidance of doubt, it should be enacted that any such defence as does exist is abolished. On the other hand, the Law Commission favours the retention of the defence of duress and its extension to all offences, including murder as a principal in the first degree. I am now concerned with the existing law. Duress is not, since *Howe and Bannister*,[14] a defence to murder, whether as a principal in the first degree or as a secondary party, and possibly not a defence to attempted murder either. But it is a defence to offences generally, including some, though probably not all, forms of treason. So, if the principles are the same, we may legitimately argue that necessity is also a defence to the same extent as duress to offences generally. Are the principles the same? Lord Simon of Glaisdale thought so in his speech in *Lynch's case*. He said[15]:

> "The only difference is that in duress the force constraining the choice is a human threat, whereas in 'necessity' it can be any circumstances constituting a threat to life (or, perhaps, limb). Duress is, thus considered, merely a particular application of the doctrine of necessity: see Glanville Williams, *Criminal Law [The General Part]* (2nd ed. 1961) 760."

Lord Simon was dissenting, though this in no way invalidated his opinion at the time it was given and, in any event, it

---

[13] Report on Defences of General Application (Law Com. No. 83, 1977).
[14] [1987] A.C. 1.
[15] [1975] A.C. 653 at p. 692.

is vindicated by *Howe and Bannister* where the House over-ruled *Lynch*, preferring the opinion of the dissenting judges, Lord Simon and Lord Kilbrandon. And, as we have seen, both Lord Hailsham and Lord Mackay thought that to hold that duress was a defence to a person charged with murder would be to overrule *Dudley and Stephens* which decided that necessity could not be a defence to a person charged with murder as a principal in the first or second degree. Even if necessity and duress are different defences they are, in some respects at least, governed by the same basic principles.

This is the line taken by the Law Commission's codifica-tion team in their Report of the Codification of the Criminal Law,[16] though it has yet to receive the approval of the Law Commission themselves. If the threat of death or serious injury is a sufficient excuse for committing a particular crime, it should make no difference whether the threat is a threat by a person, "Commit that crime—or else, . . . " or takes some other form. The effect on the person threatened is the same.

Duress of Circumstances

As the result of very recent developments in the law, we now seem to have reached that position, though more or less by accident. In the case of *Willer*[17] in 1987 the defendant was charged with reckless driving after he had driven very slowly on a pavement in order to escape from a gang of youths who were obviously intent on doing violence to him and his pas-sengers. At the trial, the defendant relied on a defence of necessity but the judge refused to leave any such defence to the jury. The Court of Appeal quashed Willer's conviction. They held that it ought to have been left to the jury to say whether the defendant drove "under that form of compulsion,

[16] Law Com. No. 143, pp. 119–121 (1985).
[17] (1986) 83 Cr.App.R. 225.

i.e. under duress." So they treated the case as simply an instance of the well-recognised defence of duress. But the defence raised was not the defence of duress as traditionally understood. When that defence has been applied, the threat has invariably taken the form, "Do this [*i.e.* commit a crime] or else . . . " The threatener wants to compel the threatened person to commit a crime. But the youths threatening Willer were not seeking to compel him to drive on the pavement, they were not saying to him, "Drive on the pavement, or else . . . " On the contrary, if they wanted to catch him and driving on the pavement was his way of escape, this was something they did not want him to do. So it was not truly a case of duress in the traditional sense. A closer analogy is with private defence. But it is better regarded as a case of necessity. If the defendant drove on the pavement to escape from a threat of death or serious bodily harm, it should really make no difference whether the threat arose from a gang of youths, a herd of charging bulls, a runaway lorry or a flood.

The true nature of the defence has been recognised by the Court of Appeal in a subsequent case, *Conway*,[18] also concerned with reckless driving. A passenger in the appellant's car, Tonna, had been the target of an attack on another vehicle a few weeks earlier, when another man was shot and Tonna was chased and narrowly escaped. On the occasion which was the subject of the appeal, two young men in civilian clothes came running towards the appellant's parked car and Tonna shouted hysterically, "Drive off." The appellant drove off because he feared a fatal attack on Tonna. The car was chased by two men in an unmarked vehicle. Apart from this alleged emergency, his manner of driving might well have been described as reckless and, of course, the jury had convicted him of reckless driving. The appellant relied on *Willer*, by which the Court of Appeal held that they were bound in relation to duress; but, this time, the court, unlike

---

[18] [1988] 3 W.L.R. 1238.

the court in *Willer*, was clearly aware that it was not concerned with the defence of duress in its traditional sense. It was convenient, Woolf L.J. said, to refer to the defence raised as "duress of circumstances"; and this he rightly treated as a variety of necessity. Like duress by threats, the defence was to be available only when the defendant could be said to be acting in order to avoid the imminent danger of death or serious injury. It seems probable that the application of the defence in *Willer* was due to a misapprehension as to the nature and extent of the traditional defence of duress, but the case was not decided *per incuriam* and was treated by the court in *Conway* as a binding precedent. This is why I suggested that the development of the defence of duress of circumstances was, to some extent, an accident, though a happy accident.

It seems probable, therefore, that duress of circumstances, like duress by threats, is a defence to crimes generally, but not a defence to murder, or perhaps attempted murder. It applies not only to an act done for the preservation of one's own life and safety but also to an act done to protect another—probably any other person who is in peril. It does not appear that there was any relationship between Conway and Tonna, other than that of driver and passenger. The case is therefore of considerable importance. Consider the following hypothetical case put by Lord Denning in *Buckoke* v. *Greater London Council*[19]:

> "A driver of a fire engine with ladders approaches the traffic lights. He sees 200 yards down the road a blazing house with a man at an upstairs window in extreme peril. The road is clear in all directions. At that moment the lights turn red. Is the driver to wait for 60 seconds or more, for the lights to turn green? If the driver waits for that time, the man's life will be lost."

[19] [1971] 1 Ch. 655, at p. 668.

Lord Denning accepted the opinion of both counsel in that case that the driver would commit an offence if he crossed the red light. Necessity would be no answer to a charge of breaking the Road Traffic Regulations. But would it be the same now that the courts have discovered the defence of duress of circumstances? The threat to the fictional man at the upstairs window seems to be no less than the threat to the passenger in Conway's car. The necessity for immediate action is no less. If we have to look for some relationship between the defendant and the person rescued, that between a fireman and a person imperilled by a fire is surely enough— the fireman probably has a duty to do all that he lawfully and reasonably can to rescue any member of the public. But it is thought that the better view is that no special relationship is necessary. Suppose that Mr. Tonna had leapt into the car of a perfect stranger, screaming that he was about to be shot. Would not the stranger be excused, no less than Mr. Conway, for any infringement of the letter of the law which reasonably appeared to him to be necessary to save a man from being murdered? Should a private citizen, driving a van with a long ladder, be less deserving of excuse than a fireman because he crossed the red light to make a rescue? I submit, not.

Perhaps Lord Denning would not be displeased by this result. He was applying the law as he believed it then to be; but he said of his hypothetical fire engine driver who crossed the red light: he "should not be prosecuted. He should be congratulated." It has always seemed to me very odd that the great Master of the Rolls should find that this conduct was both a breach of the criminal law and a case for congratulation. Plainly, he thought that, from a moral point of view, the driver's conduct was not only excusable but justifiable. Consider also the case of *Kitson*[20] where it was held that a person had no defence to a charge of driving while impaired

[20] (1955) 39 Cr.App.R. 66.

by drink when he had been sleeping in a car driven by
another, awoke to find the car running down a hill, and
"drove" by steering the car to safety. If the only danger was
to property—the car itself, or perhaps a fence that it was
about to run into—there would still be no defence, even after
Willer and *Conway*; but, if there was danger of death or
serious injury to the defendant or another person, there
would now appear to be duress of circumstances. What
indeed, would we think of a person who, finding himself in
such a situation, allowed the car to continue its career and
run over and kill or seriously injure a child? Would not the
Common People regard the failure to steer the car, rather
than the steering of it, to safety, when that could easily be
done, as "criminal"? What if the driver was a lawyer whose
reply was that, in keeping his hands off the steering wheel, he
was only doing what the Court of Criminal Appeal had said
he must do? I believe we would all say, like Lord Denning of
the fire engine driver, that, if that was the law, he ought to
have disobeyed the law and would merit congratulations for
doing so.

It is possible that, as a result of *Willer* and of *Conway* we
have got away from that particular absurdity but it is impossible to be completely confident about this. Take the case of
the fireman. At the time when *Bucocke's case* was decided
there was a statutory exemption from obeying speed limits
for ambulances, police cars and fire engines on the way to
emergencies,[21] but no such exemption from obeying traffic
lights. This might be taken to suggest that Parliament
intended that there should be no exemption from traffic
lights. Such an argument depends on the fiction that the statute book, including statutory instruments, is written as a consistent whole. As a matter of fact, this is far from being the
case but that does not necessarily preclude a theoretical argument on those lines. Following and, no doubt as a result of,

---

[21] Road Traffic Regulation Act 1967.

Buckoke's case, a statutory instrument has provided a similar exemption for ambulances, police and firemen in respect of traffic lights.[22]

Suppose, now, that the person held up at the traffic lights is not a fireman but a contractor with a long ladder on his lorry. Otherwise, the circumstances are just as envisaged in Lord Denning's dramatic example. Does the contractor commit an offence if he crosses the lights to save the man at the upstairs window? If he pleads duress of circumstances and relies on *Willer* and *Conway* he may be met with the argument that Parliament has provided that ambulance men, police and firemen may cross the lights in these circumstances and that the plain implication of that legislation is that no one else may do so. If anyone can do it, why has Parliament made this special provision? Parliament must be taken to know the law. Statutory provision for particular cases may pose difficulties for the development by the courts of general principles. It is a formidable argument but not, I hope, conclusive. First, the proposition that Parliament knows the law is a blatant legal fiction; secondly, the form of the legislation is, for all practical purposes, settled, not in Parliament but in a Ministry, and no one pretends that Ministers and their advisers know all the law; and, thirdly, the common law, though theoretically existing unchanged from time immemorial, is in fact, as everyone knows (and as Lord Hailsham judicially recognised in a passage I quoted earlier[23]) being developed by the courts. So that argument against recognising the general effect of a defence of duress of circumstances depends entirely on fictions which should not be allowed to stand in the way of desirable developments in the law.

[22] The Traffic Signs Regulations and General Directions 1975 (S.I. 1975 No. 1536), reg. 34(1)(b).
[23] Above, p. 2.

Threats to Damage Property or Financial Interests

If that is right, it is satisfactory as far as it goes, but it leaves us with a pretty limited defence of duress, whether by threats or of circumstances. Only threats of death or serious bodily harm are enough. Threats of damage to property or to cause other injuries, however grave, and however enormous the threatened injury in relation to any harm that might flow from the commission of the crime, do not excuse its commission. At least, there is no authority that such threats excuse and some authority against; but it may be that the way is not closed to the further development of this defence. It is true that in *Lynch's case*[24] Lord Simon regarded a rule that only a threat of bodily harm could amount to duress as one point in a very uncertain area of the law which might be taken to be settled. He went on:

> "But a threat to property may, in certain circumstances, be as potent in overbearing the actor's wish not to perform the prohibited act as a threat of physical harm. For example, the threat may be to burn down his house unless the householder merely keeps watch against interruption while a crime is committed. Or a fugitive from justice may say, 'I have it in my power to make your son bankrupt. You can avoid that merely by driving me to the airport.' Would not many ordinary people yield to such threats, and act contrary to their wish not to perform an action prohibited by law? Faced with such an anomaly, is not the only answer, 'Well, the law must draw a line somewhere; and, as a result of experience and human valuation, the law draws it between threats to property and threats to the person.' "

Lord Simon recognises that this is an anomaly; and there is

[24] [1975] A.C. 653 at pp. 686–687.

of course another possible answer, which is to remove the anomaly. There is no authority binding on the House of Lords to the effect that threats to property cannot be a sufficient duress to found a defence to any charge of crime. The only case his Lordship cites is that of *M'Growther*[25] in 1746 in which it was held that a threat to burn the defendant's house and drive off his cattle was not a defence to a charge of treason. "The only force that doth excuse," said Lee C.J., "is a force upon the person and present fear of death." But treason was regarded as the gravest crime in the criminal calendar. It does not follow that a threat to burn the defendant's house and destroy his property cannot found a defence to a charge of other, less grave, crimes.

The Criminal Damage Act 1971, section 5(2)(*b*), provides that the fact that the defendant acted "in order to protect property belonging to himself or another" may be a lawful excuse for intentionally or recklessly damaging property belonging to another. The person who acts because a threat has been made to damage or destroy his or another's property if he does not do so, acts "in order to protect property." If his act is one of criminal damage, he may rely on the statutory defence provided by this section; but why, in principle, should this defence be confined to offences of criminal damage? Suppose that Edward has thrown petrol over the front door of Dan's house and is threatening to set fire to it unless Dan (i) breaks the window of Peter's car which is parked in the drive and (ii) takes from the car a parcel containing heroin. Dan thinks discretion the better part of valour and does as he is instructed. If he is charged with criminal damage to Peter's car, he may rely on the statutory defence and claim that he acted in order to protect his house, which he believed was in immediate need of protection, and that the means of protection adopted were reasonable in the circumstances; but, if he is charged with being in possession of

---

[25] (1746) Fost. 13.

heroin, or aiding and abetting Edward's possession of heroin, there is no statutory defence available. If the threat of damage to the house was sufficient to exempt him from liability for criminal damage, why should it not be enough to exempt him from liability for the drugs offences? Only an extension of the defence of duress, as it is currently stated, could excuse him. It is not beyond the powers of the courts to make such an extension, if they should be so minded. The situation, as it at present appears to be, is a typical result of the haphazard way in which English law develops; but, by passing the Criminal Damage Act, Parliament has acknowledged that a threat to a person's property may be a sufficient excuse in law for his commission of what would otherwise be a crime. In a Criminal Damage Act, this was naturally confined to crimes of criminal damage, but there does not appear to be any other reason for so confining it.

The Standards Set by the Criminal Law

"We are often compelled to set up standards we cannot reach ourselves, and to lay down rules which we could not ourselves satisfy. But a man has no right to declare temptation to be an excuse, though he might himself have yielded to it, nor allow compassion for the criminal to change or weaken in any manner the legal definition of crime."

Those are the words of Lord Coleridge C.J. in *Dudley and Stephens*.[26] He asserts that the standards prescribed by the criminal law are higher than those which might be expected of the judges themselves, as individuals. Though the judges feel that they themselves would have behaved as the accused person did, had they found themselves in his situation, still

[26] (1884) 14 Q.B.D. 273, at p. 288.

they must hold his conduct to be criminal. I question whether this can be right. It is begging the question to declare that they cannot "allow compassion for *the criminal* to change or weaken in any manner *the definition of crime*," when the very issue before them is whether the person charged is a criminal and whether the definition of crime extends to his case. If a person charged has behaved as a law-abiding person of the highest integrity might well have behaved—and we must assume that Lord Coleridge and his brethren were such persons—can it be right to condemn him as a criminal? I prefer the view vividly expressed by counsel in a South African case[27] concerning duress:

> "The criminal law should not be applied as if it were a blueprint for saintliness but rather in a manner in which it can be obeyed by the reasonable man."

That argument was found persuasive by the South African court but it was expresssly rejected by Lord Hailsham L.C. in *Howe and Bannister*[28] and it is the blueprint for saintliness, or rather, heroism, theory which prevails in the English law relating to duress when it is relied on as a defence to murder. Lord Hailsham said:

> "I have known in my own lifetime of too many acts of heroism by ordinary human beings of no more than ordinary fortitude to regard a law as either 'just or humane' which withdraws the protection of the criminal law from the innocent victim and casts the cloak of its protection on the coward and poltroon in the name of a 'concession to human frailty.' "

But no one is suggesting that the "coward and poltroon" should be able to rely on the defence. It would be available only when the threats were such that, in the opinion of the

---

[27] *Goliath* 1972 (3) S.A. 1 (A.D.)
[28] [1987] A.C. 417 at p. 432.

jury, the ordinary person of reasonable fortitude, of the age and sex and with the other relevant characteristics of the defendant, *would* have yielded to the threat. Surely neither Lord Hailsham nor anyone else can really assert that no such circumstances will ever arise; but if they do, that ordinary person of reasonable fortitude will be guilty of murder. Heroism is a splendid thing but it is usually considered to be conduct going beyond the call of duty, which is why the hero is awarded a medal. A person should not be liable to life imprisonment for failing to be a hero.

It is true that the writers of authority in the criminal law have for centuries stated that duress is not a defence to murder because a man "ought to die himself rather than escape by the murder of an innocent."[29] Similarly, Lord Hailsham thought that the man who takes the life of another to save his own cannot claim that he is choosing the lesser of two evils. But all this seems to presuppose that there is a direct choice between the life of the person under duress and the life of the victim. This is by no means always the case for two reasons.

First, murder does not require an intention to kill but is satisfied by an intention to cause serious injury. The defendant may have been told—and, sadly, today this is far from being fanciful—"kneecap X"—*i.e.* fire a gun into his kneecaps so as to cause him serious injury—"or you will be killed." If the defendant does so and X dies, he may properly be charged with murder, and his only possible defence will be duress. But he was not faced with a straight choice between his life and X's. Most victims of kneecapping survive, as the barbarous perpetrators intend, as a warning to others. Dreadful though the injury is, might not a reasonable man think it a lesser evil than the loss of his own life? And is it not a threat to which the ordinary man of reasonable fortitude might yield? If he refuses and dies he may well merit the posthumous award of the George Cross, but it should surely not

---

[29] Blackstone, *Commentaries*, iv, 30.

be a crime to fail to come up to the exacting and exceptional standard of courage demanded for such an award.

Secondly, the person charged with murder may not himself have done the act of killing but may be charged with aiding, abetting, counselling or procuring the act by the killer. It is enough for the prosecution to prove that the defendant knowingly did any act of assistance. To embroider a little on an example discussed by their Lordships, suppose that a woman motorist, driving with her two children, is hijacked by a gunman who tells her, "Drive me to the barracks and stop opposite the sentry." She realises he is going to shoot the sentry and demurs. He then threatens to kill the two children unless she does so. If she complies and he kills the sentry, she has aided and abetted a murder. But even the most resolute and well-disposed citizen would be likely to yield to such a threat if it was apparently seriously intended. Is it not, indeed, very arguable that the woman *ought* to yield—that she would be foolhardy and improvident, perhaps even failing in her duty to her children, if she refused to drive on and they were shot? The choice is not even a direct one between the lives of her children and the life of the sentry—it is a choice between their lives and *a risk* to the life of the sentry. If she drives on, there is no certainty that the plan will succeed. It might be frustrated in many ways. The risk to the sentry is certainly a lesser evil than the certain death of the two children. Even if the law demanded justification, as distinct from excuse, to found the defence, (which I do not accept) here, surely, we have it.

Supplementing Defences by Administrative Remedies

Hypothetical cases such as that of the hijacked woman motorist were put in argument in the House of Lords. Lord

Griffiths's response[30] was that "The short practical answer is that it is inconceivable that such persons would be prosecuted, they would be called as the principal witness for the prosecution . . . " But is this a good answer? The fact remains that the person in question, however morally innocent, would be a murderer in law, whether prosecuted and convicted or not. If called as a witness for the prosecution, as Lord Griffiths suggests, he would be, in law, an accomplice, a murderer, and, under the blanket rule now prevailing, it would be the duty of the judge to warn the jury that it would be dangerous to convict on the uncorroborated evidence of an accomplice—even though—absurdly—it would be in order for him to add, in this case, not *very* dangerous. But the main point is that a person who, morally, is absolutely innocent, who perhaps has acted entirely as a responsible citizen ought to act, should not be in peril of conviction for murder and at the mercy of the prosecuting authority.

Both Lord Hailsham and Lord Griffiths envisaged the possibility of such a person being convicted of murder but thought that the matter could be satisfactorily dealt with by the Parole Board and the Home Secretary. Lord Griffiths also remarked that the "sentence for murder although mandatory and expressed as imprisonment for life, is in fact an indefinite sentence which is kept constantly under review. . . . " But the Criminal Law Revision Committee[31] has recently been at pains to emphasise the severity of the sentence for murder and the fact that the murderer, if released, is only on licence and is liable to recall at any time during his life. He has lost his right to his liberty, literally, for the rest of his life. Indeed, the existence of the mandatory penalty is a reason why duress should be a defence to murder which does not exist in the case of other crimes. In every

[30] [1987] A.C. 417 at p. 445.
[31] Twelfth Report, Cmnd. 5184 (1973); Fourteenth Report, Cmnd. 7844 (1980) at p. 19.

other crime the duress, if it was not a defence, could be taken into account in fixing the sentence and an absolute discharge given in appropriate cases, but this is not possible in murder.

These administrative palliatives, then, in no way compensate for the lack of a proper defence. In 1969, Lord Reid, when declining to hold that possession of controlled drugs was an offence of strict liability, said: "I dissent emphatically from the view that Parliament can be supposed to have been of the opinion that it could be left to the discretion of the police not to prosecute, or that if there was a prosecution justice would be served by only a nominal penalty being imposed."[32] Possession of controlled drugs, though in Lord Reid's opinion, "a truly criminal and disgraceful offence," is not in the same class as murder. If it is wrong to leave the innocent possessor of controlled drugs to the mercy of administrative discretion, it cannot be right so to leave the innocent participant in a murder.

Distrust of the Jury; and the Onus of Proof

The circumstances will be rare in which the killing of another, or participation in the killing of another, will be regarded by reasonable people as excusable. But to withhold even the possibility of a defence suggests to my mind a lack of confidence in the jury. Judges constantly praise the institution of jury trial but, in practice, they often reveal an unwillingness to trust it.[33] In a fairly long experience of sitting with judges on law reform bodies I have observed that the fear of "bogus defences" looms large in judicial thought. The movement from objective to subjective tests of criminal liability has often been resisted on this ground. The judge will know it is a bogus defence, of course; but the poor gullible jury

[32] *Warner* v. *Metropolitan Police Commissioner* [1969] 2 A.C. 256 at p. 278.
[33] See, *e.g. Kearney* [1988] Crim.L.R. 530 and commentary.

may fail to detect it. The House of Lords in *Howe* recognise the there may be cases of murder under duress which do not deserve punishment but they would rather trust the administrative authorities to make the distinction than the jury.

Related to this point is the matter of onus of proof. It is well-settled that, once some evidence of duress (or any other defence at common law except insanity) is given, the onus of proof is on the prosecution to prove beyond reasonable doubt that at least one of the conditions of the defence is not made out. That is the effect of the decision of the House of Lords in *Woolmington* v. *D.P.P.*[34] (1935) as subsequently interpreted and applied. Judges might more readily accept a defence, or a more broadly based defence, if the onus of proof were on the defendant. This was one of the considerations expressed by the Lord Chief Justice in the Court of Appeal in *Howe and Bannister*.[35] In *Sweet* v. *Parsley*[36] Lord Reid thought that "one of the bad effects of the decision in *Woolmington* v. *D.P.P.*" may have been to discourage the development of "a halfway house" between absolute liability and the requirement of full *mens rea*. It is possible that another "bad effect" has been to hinder the proper development of defences. The best is sometimes said to be the enemy of the good and this may be an instance of that phenomenon; but the principle of *Woolmington* is, in my opinion, of such fundamental importance that we must put up with such "bad effects" as we cannot avoid.

[34] [1935] A.C. 462.
[35] *Burke, Clarkson, Howe and Bannister*.
[36] [1970] A.C. 132 at p. 150.

4. Private Defence and the Prevention of Crime

A farmworker, suspected of being a terrorist, is questioned by soldiers and dismissed. He walks away. Then the soldiers change their minds. One of them goes to call him back and, when he is eight yards away, calls on him to stop. The man starts to run away. The soldier immediately takes aim with his rifle and shoots him in the back, killing him. It turns out that the dead man was not a terrorist but an innocent person. The soldier is found not guilty of murder. He has committed no offence.

I suggested in my first lecture, when discussing the wounding of Stephen Waldorf, that today it will rarely if ever be permissible to kill or wound, simply in order to make an arrest. That very evening I saw depicted by actors on television[1] the scene I have described, followed by the assertion that, following Lord Diplock's pronouncements on that case, soldiers have carte blanche to use as much force as they want to, whenever they want to; and that the use of force is regarded as reasonable, even to prevent someone running away. Was I then misleading you, the Common People, whom Miss Hamlyn wished to enlighten? I think not. Such a

---

[1] "Panorama," B.B.C., October 17, 1988.

reconstruction can be very misleading. The case, if I have identified it correctly, is the *Att.-Gen. for Northern Ireland's Reference (No. 1 of 1975)*[2] and the first thing to observe about it is that the House of Lords decided no point of law, the question whether force used in the prevention of crime is reasonable or not being one of fact. But Lord Diplock's dicta are important and it is necessary to try to determine the situation to which they related. The Attorney-General put it as follows[3]:

> "What is relevant to the issue of lawful or unlawful killing is what the accused honestly and reasonably believed to be the likely result of the man getting away *in terms of his committing an immediate act of terrorism.*"

And Lord Diplock, in whose speech a majority of the House of Lords concurred, said[4]:

> "It has not been suggested that shooting to kill or seriously wound would be justified in attempting to effect the arrest under section 12 [of the Northern Ireland (Emergency Provisions) Act 1973] of a person who, though he was suspected of belonging to a proscribed organisation (which constitutes an offence under section 19) was not also believed on reasonable grounds to be likely to commit actual crimes of violence if he succeeded in avoiding arrest."

But does this then mean that, as suggested in the programme, the soldier was entitled to shoot because he believed the man to be a terrorist who, if he escaped, would live *to fight another day*? I submit not. That would indeed give soldiers the right to execute persons reasonably suspected of

---

[2] [1977] A.C. 105. The trial judge, MacDermott J., was not satisfied that the defendant had an intent to kill or cause grievous bodily harm. He may have acted instinctively without foreseeing the likely consequences.

[3] *Ibid.* at p. 110.

[4] *Ibid.* at p. 137.

belonging to terrorist organisations. It would be contrary to a basic principle that the harm to be prevented must be imminent. It is true that Lord Diplock said that he would deal with the reference "on the basis that the accused's honest and reasoonable belief was that the deceased was a member of the I.R.A. who, if he got away, was likely *sooner or later* to participate in acts of violence"; but it is most important to notice that he also said[5]:

> "In the facts that are to be assumed for the purposes of the reference there is material upon which a jury might take the view that the accused had reasonable grounds for the *apprehension of imminent danger to himself and other members of the patrol* if the deceased were allowed to get away and join armed fellow-members of the Provisional I.R.A. who might be lurking in the neighbourhood and that the time available to the accused to make up his mind what to do was so short that even a reasonable man could act only intuitively."

That was the case which the court had under consideration, whatever actually happened on the day. If the shooting was to be justified or excused, it was not on the ground that it was necessary in order to make an arrest, or, I would submit, in order to prevent the escape of a man who might be a danger at some unknown time in the future, but on the ground that it may have appeared to the soldier to be necessary to prevent *imminent danger* to the lives of himself and his comrades. The law is the same for soldiers, S.A.S. or not, as it is for civilians—that indeed was the source of bitter complaint in the same programme by Lieutenant-Colonel Charles Wakerley.

It is a cardinal principle that the use of force against another, by soldier or civilian, can be justified or excused only if it was *both* necessary and reasonable. It may be

[5] *Ibid.* at p. 135.

necessary to shoot in order to make an arrest; but if, on the facts known to the defendant, it is not reasonable to do so, the shooting is unlawful.

Let me envisage a Machiavellian and purely fictitious police force who have in their possession conclusive proof that A, B and C have conspired to commit a robbery. The robbers will be armed to the teeth with deadly weapons, which they will not hesitate to use. The officers could arrest them now; but they think the world would be a better place without A, B and C; so they hold their hand, allow the plan to proceed and prepare an ambush. A, B and C walk into the trap. On being challenged, they go for their weapons—and the police marksmen shoot them down. It is both necessary and reasonable for the marksmen to shoot in order to save their own lives. They commit no offence. But it does not necessarily follow that the senior officers are exempt from criminal liability. Crime may be committed through an innocent agent. When these fictitious senior officers in this entirely hypothetical case formed the intention to kill there was no necessity to do so and, when the intended deaths occurred, that, arguably was murder.

But we must not jump too rapidly to conclusions. Until the Criminal Law Act 1977, conspiracy was not an arrestable offence and merely preparatory acts were, and are, not an offence at all. So the police had to wait until the conspirators had gone beyond mere preparation and were actually attempting to commit the crime before they could be arrested. Under the Criminal Law Act, a conspiracy to commit an arrestable offence is itself an arrestable offence; but the decision is still by no means so easy as it might look. Conspirators are rarely so obliging as to allow their plotting to be seen or heard. The usual way of proving a conspiracy is not direct evidence of an agreement but proof that the defendants so acted in concert as to compel the conclusion by a jury that they were acting in pursuance of a prior agreement to commit the crime alleged. So the police may still have to wait until the supposed conspirators begin to put their plan into execution. That is a matter for the professional judgment of the police at the time, not of the courts after the event, and the opinion has been stated (in a rather different context, it is true) by a former Lord Chancellor, Lord Cave, that "a court which attempted to review such a decision from the point of view of its wisdom or prudence would . . . be exceeding its proper functions."[6] But, even if the officers were guilty of an error of judgment, that would not involve criminal liability unless it was proved that the decision was made recklessly— and then they might be liable for manslaughter or unlawful wounding.

Reasonable Force and Reasonable Belief

Claims that force was used in private defence or the prevention of crime commonly arise out of situations of turmoil and confusion. In such circumstances it is very easy to make a mistake of fact. A person may suppose that he or another is being attacked, or is about to be attacked, when this is not so; or he may suppose that a weapon is being used against him or another, or is about to be used, when this is not so.

It may be that the force used would have been reasonable, and therefore lawful, had the facts been as the person using the force thought them to be; but, on the actual facts, it was not necessary to use any force, or the amount of force used was unreasonable. Where does he stand if he is charged with an offence of assault, or wounding, or even homicide?

You will have noticed that in the passages I have read from the *Att.-Gen. for Northern Ireland's Reference* counsel and Lord Diplock referred to *reasonable* belief. For many years, it was thought to be the law that a person could rely on such a

---

[6] *Glasbrook Bros. Ltd.* v. *Glamorgan County Council* [1925] A.C. 270 at p. 281.

mistake of fact only if it was based on reasonable grounds. This was stated in many cases. For example, in the case of *Rose*[7] in 1884, the defendant, a man of about 22, was charged with the murder of his father, a very powerful man, given to excessive drinking, who had on more than one occasion threatened to kill his wife. On the night in question he was attacking his wife at the top of the stairs and her daughters were shouting "Murder." The defendant came running from his room and shot and killed his father. Lopes J. told the jury that if the defendant "honestly believed, and had reasonable grounds for the belief, that his mother's life was in imminent peril, and that the fatal shot which he fired was absolutely necessary for the preservation of her life," then he was to be excused; but if he had not such a belief . . . or had not reasonable grounds for such a belief," then he was guilty of murder. The jury acquitted the defendant so we must assume that they found that he had reasonable grounds for his belief that his mother's life was in imminent peril. But, if they had been satisfied that his belief, though perfectly genuine, was not based on reasonable grounds, they would, if they had obeyed the judge's instruction, have convicted him of murder—then, of course, a capital offence.

That may seem to you, as it certainly does to me, a very harsh doctrine. For a person acting in good faith to defend another and to prevent crime, conviction of murder and the imposition of the death sentence (whether carried out or not) seems a high price to pay for making an unreasonable mistake. But until 1983 it was consistently stated that an honest belief was no answer to a charge unless it was based on reasonable grounds. In a case in the Divisional Court in 1980, *Albert* v. *Lavin*,[8] Hodgson J. reviewed the law and cited several similar statements. In particular, in the very important decision of the House of Lords, *D.P.P.* v.

---

[7] (1884) 15 Cox C.C. 540.
[8] (1980) 72 Cr.App.R. 178.

Morgan,[9] in 1975 the three Law Lords who referred, *obiter*, to the matter of self-defence all said that a mistaken belief could be relied on only if it was based on reasonable grounds. But in *Albert* v. *Lavin* Hodgson J., to his own surprise as well as that of others, was unable to find any direct authority on this matter—that is, he found no case of a person who acted, as he believed, in self-defence or defence of another, and was convicted because his belief was mistaken and unreasonable. Nevertheless, the Divisional Court felt obliged to follow the consistent dicta, though with obvious reluctance.

Two years later in 1983 in the case of *Williams (Gladstone)*[10] the Court of Appeal boldly rejected that long line of dicta, including the remarks of the Law Lords, and held that the common law is, and therefore always has been, that a defendant relying on private defence is to be judged on the facts as he honestly believed them to be, whether his belief was reasonable or not. The appellant in that case had been convicted of an assault occasioning actual bodily harm to a man called Mason. His story was that, as he was returning from work on a bus, he saw Mason, whom he did not know, dragging a youth along and striking him again and again. He got off the bus, went to the youth's assistance and punched Mason to save the youth from further beating. Mason's evidence was that, having seen the youth snatch a handbag, he had caught him and was taking him to the police station. Bag-snatching is probably robbery and is at least theft, an arrestable offence, and, if, as we must assume, the theft had actually been committed, Mason, like anyone else, was entitled to arrest the thief, using reasonable force if that was necessary, and to deliver him into the custody of the police. So it was alleged that Mason was assaulted while exercising his lawful rights as a citizen. But Williams did not know anything about the alleged bag-snatching incident. He claimed

[9] [1976] A.C. 182.
[10] (1984) 78 Cr.App.R. 276.

that all he saw was Mason beating the youth and that he intervened to prevent an unlawful assault. The trial judge directed the jury that Williams had a defence to the charge if he believed *on reasonable grounds* that Mason was acting unlawfully. The jury convicted him. The Court of Appeal quashed his conviction on two grounds, the first of which is not relevant here. The second ground was that the jury had been misdirected on private defence. Lord Lane C.J. said:

"The reasonableness or unreasonableness of the defendant's alleged belief is material to the question of whether the belief was held by the defendant at all. If the belief was in fact held, its unreasonableness, so far as guilt or innocence is concerned, is neither here nor there. It is irrelevant. Were it otherwise, the defendant would be convicted because he was negligent in failing to recognise that the victim was not consenting or that a crime was not being committed and so on."

The Lord Chief Justice referred to the Fourteenth Report of the Criminal Law Revision Committee[11] in 1980 and quoted its recommendation that "The common law of self-defence should be replaced by a statutory defence providing that a person may use such force as is reasonable in the circumstances as he believes them to be in the defence of himself or any other person." This recommendation has never been implemented by Parliament but his Lordship asserted that the rule stated in the recommendation represents the present common law. That was no doubt a surprise, though probably not an unwelcome one, to the members of the Committee, including the distinguished judges who sat on it. *Williams (Gladstone)*, in my opinion, is one of the most remarkable instances of judicial law reform in modern times, rejecting, as it did, a long-standing and apparently unanimous statement of the law, not only in England but in the

---

[11] Cmnd. 7844 (1980), at pp. 119–122.

common law world generally. There was doubt whether the new statement of the law would survive. Some considered the proposition about self-defence to be an *obiter dictum* only, the *ratio decidendi* of the case being found in the first reason given; but it was soon followed in other decisions of the Court of Appeal where the proposition was the *ratio decidendi*; and then, most importantly, it received the approval of the Privy Council in *Beckford* v. *R.*,[12] a decision of a Judicial Committee so composed that it probably represents the opinion of the House of Lords.

Reasonable Force Only

It must be emphasised that the defendant is still entitled to use only reasonable force. If he uses force which, even on the facts as he believes them to be, is unreasonable, then he commits an offence. It is no answer for him say, with truth, that he thought the force he used was reasonable in the circumstances. It is for the law, that is, in practice, the jury or magistrates, to decide how much force it is reasonable to use in particular circumstances. I believe that this is the right principle because it would be impracticable to allow everyone to decide for himself how much force is appropriate. You may think that this creates a grave difficulty for any person who is about to use force to prevent crime or to defend himself or another. How can he judge what degree of force some jury or bench of magistrates at some date in the quite distant future, and in the cool and detached atmosphere of a courtroom, might think it reasonable that he should use? It is a criticism that is often voiced and it has some force; but the position is not in fact as bad as it seems.

First, the standard of judgment required of a person in this

[12] [1987] 3 W.L.R. 611.

situation is not a strict one. There is a famous dictum of the great American judge, Oliver Wendell Holmes[13] that—

"Detached reflection cannot be demanded in the presence of an uplifted knife,"

and our own Lord Chief Justice has said[14]—

"In the circumstances one did not use jeweller's scales to measure reasonable force."

Secondly, to quote Lord Morris of Borth-y-Gest, speaking in 1971 for the Privy Council in *Palmer*[15]:

"If a jury thought that in a moment of unexpected anguish a person attacked had only done what he honestly and instinctively thought was necessary that would be most potent evidence that only reasonable defensive action had been taken. A jury will be told that the defence of self-defence, where the evidence makes its raising possible, will only fail if the prosecution show beyond doubt that what the accused did was not done by way of self-defence."

So, if a person was acting in good faith in defence of himself or another, it is improbable that he will be convicted even though, in retrospect, it appears that he may have used more force then was necessary in the light of the circumstances as he believed them to be. But there must be some limits. If a small, 10-year-old boy attacks a robust, six-feet-tall man with his fists, it cannot be lawful for the man to repel the boy's attack by splitting his skull with an axe. So, inevitably, an objective test of reasonableness has to be applied. It is doubtful if it is possible to do better, in the present state of the law, than to apply such a test in the manner described by Lord Morris.

[13] *Brown* v. *United States*, 256 U.S. 335.
[14] *Reed* v. *Wastie* (1972) *The Times*, February 10, 1972.
[15] [1971] 1 All E.R. 1077 at p. 1088.

But should not the law be changed so as to be more informative, so that the citizen can be clear about what he can and cannot do in private defence or the prevention of crime? For example, is a woman threatened with rape justified or excused in killing her assailant if that is the only way in which she can prevent the rape taking place? According to a report in *The Times* for October 1, 1987, Judge Hazan (later Hazan J.) directed the jury to return a verdict of not guilty where a woman, Mrs. Clugstone, was charged with murder when she had killed a man by stabbing him with a penknife after he had raped her and she was defending herself against further attack. The judge told the jury that there was no real evidence to contradict the defendant's account of the matter which was that she was defending herself. If the act had been done out of revenge and not to repel a further attack it would have been unlawful and the killing would probably have been murder. The judge presumably took the view that, on the particular facts of that case, no reasonable jury could have been satisfied beyond reasonable doubt that the defendant used unnecessary or unreasonable force. But the judge warned, "My ruling in this case is not to be regarded in any way as a charter for victims of serious assaults, even rape victims, to kill their assailants"; and he said that the police and the Director of Public Prosecutions were not at fault in bringing the prosecution for murder.

Force Used in the Protection of Property

If the woman threatened with rape is in a dilemma, so too is the householder faced by a burglar. I heard a former deputy Chief Constable state on television recently that when a burglar crossed his window sill, he took the view that the burglar had forfeited his civil rights. My heart goes along with that, but not my head. It is true that in 1893, a distinguished judge, Willes J., said, extra-judicially,[16] that the householder who came down in the night and found a burglar packing up his property should load a double-barrelled shot gun, take careful aim at the burglar's back and, without attracting his attention, pull both triggers. That advice should be regarded with equal scepticism. Readers of Kenny's *Outlines of Criminal Law*[17] will recall that, in one of his memorable footnotes, he told us of a Mr. Purcell of County Cork, a septuagenarian, who was knighted in 1911 for killing four burglars with a carving knife. The killer of a burglar today is more likely to find himself in the dock than at an investiture in Buckingham Palace. Burglars do not, of course, forfeit all their civil rights. The householder is entitled by section 3 of the Criminal Law Act 1967 to use reasonable force to prevent the commission of the crime of burglary or of theft and to arrest the offender but I very much doubt if it would be regarded as reasonable to kill him simply to stop him getting away with your video recorder or even some unique and highly-prized possession like an engagement ring.

The lawfulness of force used in the protection of property is, if anything, even vaguer than the corresponding law relating to the protection of the person, but it is clearly very limited. In the case this year of *Iddenden*[18] the defendant was the owner of a property which had been the subject of repeated thefts and break-ins. Between April 1986 and February 24, 1987 he made no less than 10 complaints to the police and these were not the only occasions on which thefts and break-ins occurred. He suffered damage to the extent of some £20,000. On February 24, 1987 the defendant found that some tiles had been stripped from the roof of his cottage. He complained to the police about their inadequate

---

[16] *The Saturday Review*, November 11, 1983, at p. 534.

[17] 17th ed., at p. 129, Footnote 4.

[18] Unreported, Court of Appeal, Criminal Division, No. 6742/G3/87, June 10, 1988.

response to his earlier complaints and threatened to take the law into his own hands and shoot anyone he found there. The police cautioned him against doing so. That night, the thieves returned. The defendant shone a torch at a man on the roof who threw a tile at him. Iddenden fired one barrel of his shotgun and wounded the thief in the ankle. The man got to the ground and ran away. Iddenden fired again and wounded him in his thigh and calf.

Iddenden was acquitted of the very serious offence of wounding with intent to cause grievous bodily harm but convicted of unlawful wounding and sentenced to two-and-a-half years' imprisonment. He had been prepared to plead guilty to unlawful wounding, presumably on advice that he had no defence to that charge, and appealed only against sentence. The Court of Appeal reduced his sentence to 12 months' imprisonment. He was a man of good character and, as the court said, had been "subjected to provocation of the worst possible kind." Clearly the court was in no doubt that he had committed a very serious offence. So far as the first shot is concerned, he might possibly have had a defence of self-defence—he might well have feared that he was going to be bombarded with tiles—but the second shot could not be so justified. Presumably Iddenden's main object was to protect his property; but that property was no longer in imminent danger from the fleeing man. The only way in which the second shot could have protected his property was by its deterrent effect on the thief and other potential future predators—and it was clearly not lawful for that purpose—or by assisting in the arrest of the thief. The defendant was entitled to use reasonable force to make the arrest; but no one in the case seems to have considered that firing the shotgun could be reasonable force for that purpose.

One modern case in which the use of a firearm in defence of property was held to be lawful is that of *Hussey*[19] in 1924.

[19] (1924) 18 Cr.App.R. 160.

The defendant rented a room in Brixton. His landlord, Mrs. West, gave him an invalid notice to quit. When he refused to do so, she came with two others, armed with a hammer, a spanner, a poker and a chisel, to force their way into the room. They broke a panel of the door which Hussey had barricaded. He then fired a shotgun through the opening and wounded two of his assailants. His conviction for unlawful wounding was quashed because the judge had misdirected the jury that he was under a duty to retreat. He was under no such duty because that would be giving up his home to a trespasser, and the common law was that a man might, if necessary, kill a trespasser, who would forcibly dispossess him of his home. Iddenden's case was different because no one was seeking to dispossess him of his home—he was not occupying the cottage at the time; but it would be dangerous for an occupier to rely on *Hussey* to justify the use of such dangerous force to resist unlawful eviction today. As well as acting in defence of his home, Hussey was probably acting to prevent a crime under the statutes of forcible entry. The common law rules relating to the use of force to prevent crime have, as we have seen, been repealed by the Criminal Law Act 1967 and replaced by the rule that reasonable force may be used. The common law rules relating to force used in retaining possession of one's home have never been expressly repealed; but where the two purposes are indistinguishable, the common law and statutory rules cannot both apply, if they are inconsistent; and the statutory rule must prevail. It is improbable that Hussey's act would be held to be the use of reasonable force today.

How Might the Law be More Informative?

How might the law do more to define the rights of the citizen in these matters? The American Model Penal Code has a section (3.04) dealing with force used in self-protection, which provides:

"The use of deadly force is not justifiable under this Section unless the actor believes that such force is necessary to protect himself against death, serious bodily harm, kidnapping or sexual intercourse compelled by force or threat."

It will be noted that this section says in express terms when deadly force is not justifiable, not when it is justifiable; but the implication seems to be that deadly force *is* justifiable if it is necessary to prevent the commission of one of the harms listed in the section. This is so irrespective of any special circumstances of the particular instance of the apprehended harm. Such a section therefore assumes that any example of any of the listed harms must be so grave as to justify the use of deadly force if that is necessary to prevent it.

Let us take the emotive case of rape. It is often said that there is no such thing as a not very serious case of rape. Suppose that a man is having sexual intercourse with a woman with her free consent, perhaps at her invitation. She decides she has had enough and tells him to withdraw. He declines to do so. That, according to the decision of the Privy Council in *Kaitamaki v. R.*,[20] is rape. Of course, the man is at fault but is it really to be said that the woman would be justified in killing him? That is an extreme case and prosecutions for such a rape are likely to be very rare, but instances of late withdrawal of consent before intercourse actually begins are probably much more common and more likely to result in prosecution. Such a case is vastly different from an attack on a woman by a stranger in a dark alley. The fact is that rape, like every other crime, varies greatly in seriousness, according to the circumstances. In the worst cases, the woman may well be justified in using deadly force to repel her assailant, but it seems to be going too far to lay down that, as a matter

[20] [1985] A.C. 147, P.C.

of law, she might do so in every case. Apart from the case of rape, this is true of the other harms listed in the section. I imagine that a broken arm is serious bodily harm, but should the law declare that a person is always justified in killing to prevent the unlawful breaking of his own or another's arm? It seems to me at least highly debateable. The Criminal Law Revision Committee, when considering the law of offences against the person looked at provisions like that in the Model Penal Code but concluded that they were undesirable for reasons of this kind and that it was preferable to retain the simple rule requiring reasonableness in the circumstances. It may be possible, however, to fill out that rule in some respects.

The "Pre-emptive Strike"

A person is not bound to wait until he is actually attacked before using force in self-defence. If he believes that an unlawful attack is imminent then he may strike first to prevent it. The police officers, Finch and Jardine, were not acting unlawfully when they fired because they genuinely believed that the man who turned out to be Stephen Waldorf was about to shoot at them. In Mrs. Clugstone's case, Judge Hazan told the jury that she was entitled to use reasonable force to resist not only an actual, but also a threatened, attack. But the threat must be imminent. The Criminal Law Revision Committee said[21] that this was the present law, though section 3 of the Criminal Law Act 1967 does not incorporate a requirement of imminence. Some members thought an express statutory requirement was unnecessary and that it could be left to the court or jury to say whether it was reasonable to use pre-emptive force, but the majority thought it should be stated that a person is not allowed to

[21] Fourteenth Report, at pp. 120–121.

take the law into his own hands by striking before self-defence becomes necessary. A blow struck before it is necessary to strike will be unlawful and, if death results, the striker will be guilty of murder or manslaughter, depending on whether the blow was struck with intent to cause death or serious bodily harm, or only some less degree of harm, and, in the former case, whether the deceased person's conduct amounted in law to provocation.

In 1980, two sisters, Charlene and Annette Maw, were convicted of manslaughter when they killed their violent and drunken father by stabbing him with a kitchen knife.[22] On the night in question the father had assaulted and abused the sisters and their mother. He was knocked unconscious by being struck on the head with a heavy mirror. It seems that it was while their father was unconscious, and while there was no imminent danger, that the sisters agreed that, if he resorted to violence again, they would kill him. When he recovered consciousness, he resumed the violence. Charlene handed Annette a knife with which she stabbed him to death. The sisters were guilty of manslaughter and not of murder only because the jury found that they were acting under provocation and they were sentenced to three years' imprisonment, a sentence which was upheld on appeal in the case of Annette but reduced to six months in the case of Charlene. The Lord Chief Justice said that, for reasons of public safety, the court would be "doing less than its duty if it allowed this sort of offence to pass with impunity." In 1979, in Scotland, where the law appears to be similar, a Mrs. Greig was found guilty of the culpable homicide of her violent and drunken husband when she stabbed and killed him as he was sitting in a chair, probably asleep.[23] He had been drinking and,

[22] *The Times*, August 20, November 18, 19, 20, 21, 22, December 4, 5, 16, 1980.

[23] *H.M. Adv.* v. *Greig*, Gane and Stoddart, *Casebook on Scottish Criminal Law*, (2nd ed.), 364.

though he was obviously not violent at the time, the defendant gave evidence that she was afraid he would become so. A
special defence of self-defence was tabled, but withdrawn by
the judge on the ground that there was no evidence to sustain
it.

According to an American writer, in the United States
homicides by "battered women" of the man who is oppress-
ing them frequently occur while the man is sleeping or his
back is turned.[24] A television programme, *The Eleventh
Hour* (Channel 4, June 20, 1988), describes how self-defence
has recently succeeded in cases of this kind in America—
cases where a wife shot her husband as he lay asleep in bed,
because he had threatened to kill their baby when he awoke,
and even a case where a wife hired others to kill her brutal
husband. American law is basically the same as English law
and does not justify or excuse killing or causing injury to
others unless it is necessary or, at least, appears to the
defendant to be necessary; and it is not immediately obvious
how such killings could be said to be necessary or to have
appeared to the women to be necessary. There was, it
appears, plenty of opportunity to invoke the protection of
the law and the women must have known that. But it seems
that the American courts and juries may have been
influenced by psychiatric evidence that the defendants were
afflicted by a concomitant of the "battered wife syndrome"
known to the psychiatrists as "learned helplessness." The
lady who hired the contract killers does not seem to have
been exactly helpless. English courts are much more sparing
and sceptical in their reception of psychiatric evidence,
taking the view that, except in the case of the mentally
abnormal, the jury is the right, and the best, body to assess

---

[24] Elizabeth Schneider, "Equal Rights to Trial for Women: Sex Bias in the
law of Self-Defence," 15 *Harvard Civil Liberties Law Review* 623 at
p. 634.

the reactions and beliefs of defendants in criminal cases. I
think it very unlikely that we shall see such developments here.

Where the defendant killed a sleeping person, the judge
would probably be right to withdraw the defence from the
jury. The law has been criticised. Mr. Tom Harper, discussing the *Maw* case, wrote[25] of the "wholly unrealistically
restrictive view which the law takes of what is a permissible
form of self-defence . . . "; and he criticised Lawton L.J.'s
assertion that there are "ample remedies" available to those
in such a situation as were the Maw sisters through the police
and social services. But, even if it is true that the remedies
are inadequate, to hold that the deliberate killing of a sleeping or unconscious man is justified or even excused would be,
in effect, to give his victim the right to execute him; and that
surely, cannot be right.

Acts Preparatory to the Use of Force

The requirement of imminence precludes the justification or
excuse, not only of the premature use of force, but also of
preparatory acts which offend against the letter of the law
unless they are *immediately* preparatory to a justifiable or
excusable act of private defence or in the prevention of
crime. This is most vividly illustrated by the recent, much-
publicised, case of *Butler*.[26] The defendant, a man of impec-
cable character, was travelling on the London underground
carrying his Malacca sword-stick. He had bought the stick as
a substitute for one owned by his father, his hope of inherit-
ing that article having been disappointed. He carried the
stick to assist him in walking, since one of his legs was shorter

[25] (1980) 130 N.L.J. 1163.
[26] Appeal No. 5853/C1/87, June 10, 1988.

than the other. He did not carry it for self-defence and at no time before the incident which led to his trial had he thought of using it as a weapon, whether of offence or defence. During his journey on the tube train, Mr. Butler was assaulted by a drunken youth, Day, who kicked him in the face and, when he retreated, followed him, seized him round the throat and started choking him. Butler drew the sword from the stick and stabbed Day in the stomach, causing him serious injuries.

Butler was not charged with any offence against Day, no doubt because the prosecuting authority took the view that, in these circumstances, the stabbing was a lawful act of self-defence. If that was the opinion of the prosecutor, the Lord Chief Justice endorsed it. He said that the use of the sword-stick in self-defence was perfectly proper. But Butler was charged with and convicted of the offence under the Prevention of Crime Act 1953 of carrying an offensive weapon in a public place and his appeal was dismissed. The sword-stick was an offensive weapon because it was made for the purpose of causing injury to the person and to carry such a weapon in a public place without lawful excuse is an offence, whatever the purpose of the carrier. The jury found that the sword-stick was an offensive weapon, though it was probably not strictly necessary to leave that question to them, and that Butler had no reasonable excuse for carrying it. The misfortune of a "gammy leg," as Mr. Butler described it, may be a good reason for carrying a stick, but it is not a reasonable excuse for carrying a sword-stick. So he was committing an offence by carrying the stick but not by using it, in the particular circumstances which arose. If a person is violently attacked, then he may use anything which he can put his hands on to repel that attack, if such use is reasonable force in the circumstances which he believes to exist.

Since *Butler's case*, the Criminal Justice Act 1988 has been passed and by section 139 it will be an offence for a person to have with him in a public place any article which has a blade or is sharply pointed, except a folding pocket knife. So carrying a swordstick will now constitute two offences. But the 1988 Act also provides that it is a defence for the person charged to prove that he had "good reason or lawful authority for having the article with him in a public place." It is not clear why the draftsman of the Act preferred "good reason" to "reasonable excuse" or whether there is any difference between them.

Suppose that a man, being aware that unprovoked attacks are not infrequently made on passengers on tube trains, were to carry a sword-stick in order to be able to defend himself against any such attack. After all, we now know that, where there is an attack of the kind made on Mr. Butler, it is lawful to use the stick and you cannot use it if you do not have it with you. Mr. Butler might have sustained serious injuries, or even been killed, if he had not had his sword-stick. But it is very doubtful whether he would have had a "reasonable excuse" under the 1953 Act or, now, "a good reason" under the 1988 Act, if he had proved that he was carrying it for defensive purposes. We have already seen that in *Evans* v. *Hughes*[27] the court said that only "an imminent particular threat affecting the particular circumstances in which the weapon was carried" could ground a reasonable excuse. In Scotland, where the 1953 Act applies, it has been held[28] that a taxi-driver has no reasonable excuse for carrying two feet of rubber hose with a piece of metal inserted at one end, though he intends to use it only for defence against violent passengers whom Edinburgh taxi-drivers sometimes encounter at night. Parisian taxi-drivers may have found a way round this difficulty by wiring up the cushions of the rear seat to the car's battery, enabling the driver, at the touch of a concealed button, to send a short, sharp shock coursing

---

[27] [1972] 1 W.L.R. 1452, above, p. 48.
[28] *Grieve* v. *Macleod* [1967] S.L.T. 70.

through the system to the back of the customer's neck[29]; but perhaps an English court would say that the entire taxi was now an "article . . . adapted for use for causing injury to the person" and so an offensive weapon which it was unlawful for the driver to have with him.

Taxi drivers are far from being the only class of people who go in fear of being attacked. Mrs. Edwina Currie was reported recently in *The Times*[30] as saying:

> "I had a front-door key when I was fourteen. I was a Scouse lass and I was used to looking after myself. I carried a pair of scissors in my handbag . . . We girls have got to be able to look after ourselves, haven't we?"

If the 14-year old Edwina had been attacked, she may well have been justified in using her scissors in self-defence; but it is probable that she was offending against the Prevention of Crime Act by carrying them with that intent—though it would, of course, have been difficult to prove in the absence of her admission of her purpose in going thus equipped; and her remark—and the publication of it by *The Times*—seems to come dangerously close to incitement to "girls" to commit the same offence.

Thus, possession may be unlawful although the possessor has the thing for a lawful purpose. In *Att.-Gen.'s Reference (No. 2 of 1983)*[31] the defendant's shop had been damaged by rioters who stole property from it and used stones and petrol bombs against some 300 police attempting unsuccessfuly to restore order. Fearing further attack, he had the shop boarded up and painted with fire-resistant paint and he made 10 petrol bombs. He intended to use these only to protect his shop if the rioters returned. He was charged with a rather

---

[29] *The Times*, October 19, 1987.
[30] *The Times*, August 3, 1988.
[31] [1984] Q.B. 456.

strange offence under section 4(1) of the Explosive Substances Act 1883, of making an explosive substance, namely a petrol bomb, in such circumstances as to give rise to a reasonable suspicion that he had not made it for a lawful object. The shopkeeper's defence was that he had made the bombs for a lawful purpose, namely, self-defence. The trial judge rejected the submission of the prosecution that the defendant was not entitled to rely on self-defence and he was acquitted by the jury.

The Attorney-General referred the case to the Court of Appeal and argued that the judge's ruling was wrong. That court held that the trial judge was right. It was open to the jury to find that the shopkeeper had made the bombs for the reasonable protection of himself and his property, should the rioters return. Clearly, the use of petrol bombs could be reasonable force only in a case where a ferocious attack was anticipated and the defendant believed that the police would not be able to give effective protection; but that may have been the situation here. If the shopkeeper intended to use the bombs only in circumstances in which it would be lawful to do so, then it followed that he had them in his possession for a lawful object. It did not follow that the possession itself was lawful; and it seems to have been accepted that the possession was in fact an offence under another statute, the Explosives Act 1875, which prohibits the manufacture and storage of explosives except under licence. The court followed a decision of the Court of Appeal in Northern Ireland, *Fegan*,[32] that possession of a firearm for the purpose of protecting the possessor may be possession for a lawful object, even though the possession itself was unlawful, being without a licence. The young Edwina Currie undoubtedly carried her scissors for a lawful purpose but her possession of them may, nevertheless, have been unlawful.

---

[32] [1972] N.I. 80.

The court in the *Att.-Gen.'s Reference* stated[33]:

"In our judgment a defendant is not left in the paradoxical position of being able to justify acts carried out in self-defence but not acts immediately preparatory to it. There is no warrant for the submission on behalf of the Attorney-General that acts of self-defence will only avail a defendant when they have been done spontaneously."

It is lawful then to make some preparation for self-defence but the emphasis seems to be very much on *immediately* preparatory. The shopkeeper's manufacture and possession of the bombs was not "justified," notwithstanding his lawful object, for it was an offence. But, if an attack on his premises of such violence as to justify the use of the bombs had been imminent, and he had got ready to throw them, his previously unlawful possession would now apparently have been legalised. When Mr. Butler began to draw the sword from the stick which, until that moment, he had been carrying unlawfully, he ceased to be in the course of committing the offence under the Prevention of Crime Act.

Self-defence is a strictly limited defence in terms of time and circumstances, but it is surely a potential defence to all crimes. Whether it is an actual defence must turn upon whether it was reasonable to break the letter of the particular law. If I happen upon a bank robbery and, being shot at by one of the robbers, I pick up the revolver which has been dropped by a wounded policeman and, quite reasonably, fire it in self-defence, I am surely not guilty of an offence under the Firearms Act 1968, section 1, of being in possession of a firearm without holding a firearm certificate—unless I retain possession of the revolver for longer than is reasonably necessary for the purposes of self-defence or the prevention of crime. It can hardly be the law that the circumstances might justify me in, or excuse me for, killing my

[33] At p. 471.

assailant with the revolver and yet not justify or excuse my being in possession of it. At the trial of Mr. Butler for having the swordstick with him, the judge told the jury that his behaviour was like that of a man holding an unlicensed shotgun who bravely intervened in a bank robbery. If charged with possessing a shotgun without a licence, he would have no excuse. That is right so far as possession of the gun before and after the incident in the bank is concerned; but for the brief period while he was using it reasonably in the prevention of crime, his possession of it was surely no offence for he would have been justified in taking up someone else's shotgun, or anything else that it was reasonable to use, to prevent the armed robbery. If an act is justifiable or excusable because done in self-defence or the prevention of crime, that ought to be a sufficient answer to a charge of any crime alleged to be involved in the doing of the act.

A Duty to Retreat?

At common law there were complex and technical rules imposing a duty upon a person who was attacked to retreat as far as he could before standing his ground and using force, or at least deadly force. But when the Criminal Law Act 1967, section 3, provided that a person may use such force as is reasonable in the prevention of crime or of making a lawful arrest, it also abolished the rules of common law on the use of force in these circumstances. That Act did not say anything about private defence which is still governed by the common law, but there is such a large overlap between the law governing private defence and that governing the prevention of crime that the law cannot sensibly distinguish between them. This is most obvious when a person uses force in defence, not of himself, but of a third person. It is now well-recognised that the right of private defence extends to the defence of third persons generally and is not confined, as was once thought, to the defence of close relatives. You will recall that *Williams (Gladstone)* was treated by the Court of Appeal as a case of private defence although the person to whose assistance Williams came was a perfect stranger. Williams was acting in private defence; but was he not also acting, or at least intending to act, in the prevention of crime? He thought he saw an assault being committed and he jumped off the bus to prevent it. It would be no use asking Mr. Williams if he was acting in private defence or the prevention of crime. If he understood the question, he would say that he was doing both. The law cannot have two differing sets of rules governing exactly the same facts; and if there is any difference, then the statutory rule must prevail.

The question of a duty to retreat is unlikely to arise where the defendant has gone to the assistance of a third person; but the principle is the same where he himself is under attack. We naturally think of a woman defending herself against a rapist as acting in self-defence but, of course, she is also trying to prevent the crime of rape. A man defending himself against an attacker armed with a knife is acting in self-defence but he is also trying to prevent the crime of unlawful wounding or murder. Under the simple, though perhaps uninformative, rule of section 3 of the 1967 Act, the only question is whether the force used to prevent the commission of the crime is reasonable in the circumstances.[34] Was it unreasonable to stand and fight? If, even when the rule is borne in mind that "detached reflection cannot be demanded in the presence of an uplifted knife," it appears that any reasonable and prudent person could and would have retreated to avoid any bloodshed, then to stand and fight may be held to be an unreasonable use of force and an offence. But the lawfulness of standing and fighting, using

---

[34] *Bird* [1985] 2 All E.R. 513, C.A., Smith & Hogan, *Criminal Law*, (6th ed.) p. 244.

force in order to prevent the attacker achieving his object, cannot depend on whether we categorise the state of mind of the defendant as an intention to prevent crime or an intention to defend himself. The facts are the same, and the intention is the same. It is not like the case of *Finch and Jardine*[35] which turned on whether the shots were fired for the purpose of making an arrest—which would have been an unlawful intention—or for the purpose of private defence—which was lawful. An intention to make an arrest is clearly distinguishable from an intention to defend oneself or another; but an intention to defend oneself and an intention to prevent the crime apprehended are the same intention. So today, the existence or otherwise of an opportunity to retreat is simply one factor to be taken into consideration in deciding whether the defendant's use of force was reasonable, and it is immaterial whether the use of force is characterised as private defence or the prevention of crime. We have, of course, seen that private defence sometimes does not involve the prevention of crime, as where a person defends himself against an attack by one who is below the age of criminal responsibility; but it would be irrational if different principles applied and it may be assumed that the principles are the same.

Conclusion These lectures are not the place for, and I have not attempted to give, a comprehensive account of the criminal law relating to justification and excuse. I have tried to follow the spirit of the Hamlyn Trust by explaining some of the complexities of a branch of the law which is in the news almost daily and which may affect any of us at any time. That some of it is complex is undeniable and even codification could not get rid of all the difficulties. It would be fanciful to suppose that the ordinary citizen, or even a lawyer, can carry all these matters in his head. Yet, in many of the situations I have envisaged, instant action is required. The guiding

---

[35] Above, p. 20.

principle should therefore be that a person should not be guilty of a criminal offence if he has behaved as any reasonable person in his situation might be expected to behave. It is simply not possible to foresee and define in advance all the circumstances in which a reasonable person would think it justifiable, or at least excusable, to break the letter of the law. It is therefore important to maintain and encourage the judicial power to develop defences. I have suggested that a distinction between justification and excuse is of only limited value in this process but that to require justification as opposed to mere excuse to found a defence may lead to a too severe test of criminal liability. The haphazard use in criminal statutes of phrases like "without reasonable excuse," with its implication that reasonable excuse generally is not a defence, is likely to continue; but the judges will find indirect ways of allowing such a defence in some cases through the interpretation of concepts like intention, recklessness and dishonesty. Notwithstanding the setback caused by the decision in *Howe and Bannister*, there are hopeful signs of a move towards a more rational and consistent law of justification and excuse, especially in the recognition of the principle (in self-defence and the prevention of crime, though not yet in duress) that a person is to be judged on the facts as he believed them to be and the defence of duress of circumstances. *Pace* the House of Lords, the morally innocent person should not, in a question of criminal liability, be left at the mercy of administrative discretion and the fear of "bogus defences" should not deter the courts from trusting the jury. We are a long way from the general application of the principle proposed and public policy will, of course, always require some qualifications of it; but it is a direction in which this developing branch of the law could and, I believe, should move.

TABLE OF CASES

TABLE OF STATUTES

INDEX

13

63 – dualistic? intention ≠ voluntary